The Spirit of Winter Camping

A Wilderness Guide to Cold Weather Camping

Harry Drabik

Illustrated by Randall Scholes

ISBN-0-931714-24-9

Nodin Press, a division of Micawber's, Inc.
525 North Third Street,
Minneapolis, MN 55401

Printed in U.S.A. at McNaughton & Gunn, Inc., Saline, MI

To
Gordon Duffield
Canadian Scouter
&
Boots Hanson
American Scouter

Two who showed the way.

About the Author

Harry Drabik came to Northern Minnesota as a teenager, and that was the start of a life centered around nature, camping, and leadership. He has been active in the Scouting program and established a specialty guiding service for the Boundary Waters Canoe Area Wilderness. Today the author is a wilderness consultant who speaks on land-use and prehistoric topics. He lives in a cabin which he rebuilt on the shore of Lake Superior and conducts field archaeology projects for the Ontario Heritage Foundation in Canada. He is also the author of *Spirit of Canoe Camping*.

Table of Contents

Around the Protective Fire

Foreword

Years ago a friend of mine from this area got a job doing construction work in Alaska. I envied his good fortune and wished it was me who was headed north. But practical reasons kept me here, and it was several years before I saw my friend, Chet, again.

He knew of my interest in winter camping, and when he was back for a visit he looked me up. I'm sure our conversation was one of those jumpy affairs where two people attempt to sort out odd bits and pieces spanning several years of stunted communication. I know I asked numerous questions about the heated tent he'd lived in the first winter he was there.

I was trying to gather as much information as possible when Chet looked at me dead-on and said, "I'll tell you this much, Harry. I've discovered what to wear in winter if you want to stay warm."

That was what I was after. "Well, what is it? Tell me about it!" I urged him to continue.

His gaze was steady, never flickered a bit. "A hotel room," Chet said. "If you keep a hotel room wrapped around your body you won't get cold. Nothing else works as well."

I'd been had, of course, but that's not the point. What I mean to convey is the notion that winter camping is somehow obscure, impractical, a form of hardship. Many people assume there can be no pleasure in something as demanding as winter camping. They prefer the pleasant security of a snug house, the convenience of electricity, the creature comforts.

I can't argue with that. Living outdoors in winter can't compete with living indoors. They are, however, vastly different experiences, which have different purposes.

Life indoors allows one to carry on under conditions of normalcy. It's meant to be convenient, functional, practical. Within the protective shell of four walls life is governed by the society/culture that a house represents. A house is a sort of earthbound space vehicle that keeps the elements out and encloses a protected environment.

Life outdoors makes one *very* aware of that. Without the buffer of a house there is the emotional thrill of being close to nature, as well as the constant pressure of trying to stay "comfortable." The learning experience is rich. Each small detail is important and one is constantly busy doing things that make a direct, immediate contribution toward comfort and survival.

You may never actually go winter camping, and it's not important that you do. I hope, however, that this book will help make you more aware of winter clothing, outdoor recreation, and more cold weather activity in general. The cold need not be an adversary if we make wise use of our resources, both human and material. With this book I hope to encourage people to discover further meaning for winter.

Introduction

Winter camping may not be our most popular winter sport, but it has been with us for a long time. In the remote past, bands of hunter-gatherers camped throughout the seasons in order to keep themselves supplied with food and material. Early explorers on this continent did some cold weather camping, though often they'd "winter over" in one location. Trappers, European and Native American, were early winter campers, too, but they often relied on prepared or established camps spaced along their trap lines.

What we'd recognize as winter camping (involving the use of portable shelter and the daily breaking of camp in order to travel) was done either by Eskimo-Inuit people or a very few non-Indian outdoorsmen. The Boy Scout program, outdoorsman Anthony Fiala, and the outdoor writer Calvin Rutstrum, were early promoters of the sport.

Over the years, equipment improved and better transportation allowed more people to reach snowcovered wilderness. Special interests, such as climbers, sought gear to protect themselves at higher, colder elevations. Backpackers extended their "season" by camping in spring or fall, both to escape crowding and simply to enjoy more time outdoors. Today more and more campers are discovering the pleasures and rewards of winter camping.

My own interest in the sport has risen and fallen. As a boy, I was an eager winter camper for a year or two. At the time, anything to do with the outdoors was my passion. Unfortunately, camping gear in those days wasn't boy-sized or practical. In time, the size of the task discouraged me. Probably, too, I had to pay more attention to schooling, so winter camping was set aside.

I continued to jump at opportunities for camping, but these came mostly in summer. Each outing was cherished. As far as I was concerned, I only enjoyed myself when I was living close to nature. When I wasn't camping, I was searching through maps or reading books in preparation for the next time. I'd daydream about each campsite and recall something special from every one. I would visualize the campsites I had used, seeing the trees near the water, noting the color of lichen on the rock, picturing the way a loon preened itself before calling. To me, these details gave meaning to life.

In time I returned to winter camping out of what I'll call "emotional necessity." Pressure at work made the peace and stability of nature all the more necessary. In nature's chill I was able to burn away some of my frustration.

I was fortunate when I returned to winter camping. I found an excellent partner to camp with, and the timing coincided with the rising popularity of cross-country skiing. An explosion of new equipment provided many opportunities for experimentation, leading to the development of the winter program described in this book. The activity itself, the company of my friend, being close to nature—all those things combined made my return to winter camping an exciting time.

I tell my story because I know I'm not alone in my love of nature, enjoyment of friends, fascination with new camping gear, desire for an extended camping season, and enthusiasm for winter sports. This book has been written for those who share such interests.

In the chapters that follow, I have presented a discussion of equipment and techniques for winter camping. The equipment is not too unusual or overly costly, and the skill required is not beyond that of most summer campers. My desire is to make winter camping *doable*. At the very least, I hope people will use this information to extend their camping seasons.

In writing this book, I've constantly felt myself tugged in opposing directions. On the one hand, I would like to promote more winter camping by a greater number of people. On the other, I feel the necessity to stress safety and provide adequate warning of winter's power. I have tried to give ample consideration to both directions and have done my best to explain my point of view.

Nearly all of my winter camping experience comes from the Boundary Waters–Quetico country along Minnesota's border with Canada. It is an area of rugged, rolling terrain covered by boreal pine forest interspersed with lowlands and lakes. In winter, temperatures of -20° F are not uncommon, and we frequently have several feet of snow on the ground by early winter. Our winters are harsh and cold. Conditions like this are common along the United States–Canada border and in the northern states. Mountainous areas likewise experience severe winters, but every area is different. For my purposes, I must focus on the problem of dealing with subzero temperatures. In other areas you may find dampness or extreme snow volumes to be of far greater concern than extreme cold. I can only advise that you research your camping area thoroughly and then plan to deal with the worst conditions possible for the area and season.

My slant in writing is aimed at small group camping, from two to six people. Winter camping is more demanding for two people than for six because the smaller group is constantly busy with all aspects of camping. As group size increases, there is more room for relaxation because people share in the work. This is an important point, because one uses up a great deal of energy in winter. Larger groups, then, make more efficient use of human energy, but I'd stop at a group size of ten or twelve. More than that creates too many "people management" problems.

Quite a few times I've been asked, "Isn't winter camping too dangerous?" There is some danger, but it becomes too dangerous only if a person is unprepared, careless, or lacks respect for the power of deep cold. Planning, preparation, and attention to detail make winter camping safe enough for most people. My comments are, in fact, directed at making winter camping accessible to the average camper.

Still, I wouldn't be comfortable with myself if I made winter camping sound too easy. Most people, especially those from urban areas, should spend a good deal of time developing travel skills close to home. Or, for example, try cooking some meals outdoors in winter. Acts that are simple in summer can be difficult when the temperature is below zero. Or just imagine what it would be like if you had to wear mittens while putting up yor tent. Better yet, try it.

It may take years to build up enough skill and experience for winter camping. But if you master your skills slowly, you will most likely become a safe and practical winter camper. As skills become a part of you, you will develop a sense about what will and won't work. Even mistakes made along the way can make an important contribution toward getting more from the experience. Winter camping forces careful examination of all details. I suspect one learns more from a single season of winter camping than could be picked up in many seasons of summer outings.

Being prepared with the right clothing and equipment is important, but it's just as important to prepare your attitude. The stress on both body and mind is considerable. For your own sake, try to maintain a realistic attitude. That means closely considering every detail of your trip when making plans, and developing enough experience along the way to keep yourself within safe limits. Winter camping is challenging, but for every difficulty there is a corresponding benefit, at least in terms of what can be learned.

Preparing for winter camping will expose you to other people, their ideas, their experiences. That by itself can be a constructive activity for you and your friends. Putting your heads together will hopefully bring out some collective wisdom. Call on the experience of others during the important first step of planning. After that will come various trials, experiments, and skill-building sessions. Those alone can be a source of much enjoyment. Working toward becoming a serious winter camper is demanding, but it's not impossible and it is certainly rewarding. I hope this book will help you to relax with the process and allow you to see enough of what is involved so that you can join the ranks of winter campers.

Philosophy

In *The Spirit of Canoe Camping*, I told readers about the Hawk and the Mouse. Those two symbols were used to represent the pathway of canoe camping and were drawn from Native American legend.

The Hawk is associated with the East where the sun rises. With the Hawk, we rise on wings of dawning interest, receiving the first rays of knowledge. As we rise, our vision expands and we take in more and more of the world around us. In spirit, at least, every camper wishes to soar with the Hawk.

But, like the Mouse, we are earthbound. Mouse is associated with the South where things are warm and green. Mouse is an innocent, trusting little fellow who gathers seeds for food and the softest grasses for a nest. Mouse pays great attention to detail, but he lacks the far-reaching vision of Hawk. Our Mouse does not see the Hawk until too late. When the two meet, they become one—part of one another. Nothing is lost, rather, something new is generated.

The Native American model provides a way to visualize the qualities associated with the discovery and eventual mastery of canoe camping.

For winter camping, other symbols are needed, and American Indian tradition provides them as well. Starting with the East and Hawk we had spring. Mouse in the south stood for summer. Our next direction is West, for the fall season.

The Black Bear stands in the West, where the sun sets. The Bear is sometimes called "looks-within," because his long sleep can remind us of self-examination. Bear's sleep of hibernation can also remind us of death. Nature seems to die each fall, but her false death is really a time of renewal. The Bear represents fall and the ideas associated with that season.

The final direction is North, for which the season is winter. Our symbol for North is the Snowy Owl, who leaves the Arctic to enjoy our milder winters. In many ages the Owl has stood for wisdom, but in the American Indian model he is practical as well as wise. Like the Hawk, he can fly and see far, but his vision comes from night-eyes, and his wings dare to flap through the frozen midnight sky.

These two symbols, Bear and Owl, are fitting emblems for winter camping. Bear reminds us to prepare for winter and to be self-contained. Owl warns us to be both wise and practical.

There is a lesson to be learned from attending to the meaning of Bear and Owl. But the lesson is greater when all four symbols are present. Our adventure into winter with Bear and Owl is built upon our previous efforts in summer with Hawk and Mouse. The four give us a whole.

North
Owl
practical wisdom
Winter

West		East
Bear		Hawk
self examination & preparation		knowledge & vision
Fall		Spring

South
Mouse
small detail & trust
Summer

These four (and all they represent) give us the basic American Indian model of the universe and our lives within it. It is sometimes called the Hoop of Life. As a teaching tool, the Hoop is purely descriptive. It never prescribes or proscribes by using labels of right and wrong.

Each life starts at one point on the Hoop. In the course of a year, in the course of our personal growth, we will make a circuit of the Hoop. Each direction has meaning to impart. Each season prepares us to live more fully. We may go round the Hoop many times while we live, always refining and learning, attempting to master the lessons found in each direction. When we master them, we find ourselves at the Center, where there is no-direction and all-directions.

I've not yet reached the Center of my Hoop. Perhaps the Center is found only when a person leaves this life for what's to come. Of that, I am not sure. But I am sure of one thing. The American Indian model is one of the best teaching tools ever devised by any people. I cannot claim to be a master of that model, but the following lessons, which relate to winter camping, are presented as a way of showing respect and appreciation for what the model has taught me.

There are five lessons. They do not come from civilization or society—they come from hard-won experience in facing the harsh bite of winter. They even attack some of our cherished ideals, forcing an altered perspective. The lessons are as follows:

We are not unique. Frostbite will not skip over some of us. All of us are subject to fatigue. All of us exist in human bodies that are quite fragile compared to those of the animals that live in the wilderness. Each of us sees things from his or her own point of view, but because we all share that trait, it is hardly unique. If we were unique we would be isolate, the experience and friendship of others having no value for us, except out of curiosity.

We are not powerful. If you want to see power, face into a below-zero wind whipping down miles of frozen lake, or calculate how much power is required to dump a foot of snow over a hundred square miles. None of us can claim power like that. A person who respects and loves life will not throw it away by engaging in a power struggle with nature. What power we have comes from other sources; often it is a product of our human inter-action.

We are not creative. We can build, use skills, combine elements, adjust, and bounce back. We can even be inventive and imaginative. But I know of no person who has created anything. Is it reasonable for someone to say he created water because he melted snow? What we do involves something other than creation.

We are not smart. A college degree is a piece of paper. In the bush, we are all prone to exactly the same degree of humanity. In winter we are equals. Politics, counseling technique, and persuasion will not have much influence on how people function when they must pull together to face a storm. Intellectual brilliance won't stop an untimely snowfall. And even a human genius doesn't know navigation as well as the migrating birds.

We are not independent. In fact, independence is a state of being "in dependence" on the most limited resource of all . . . yourself. The harshness of winter makes human cooperation and interdependence essential tools for survival. Sharing even the most meager time in life can be enjoyable and rewarding, and I, for one, do not wish to be independent of such experiences. I'm aware that I'm dependent on food and clothing for survival, and I'm happy to be interdependent with people.

Those are the lessons. They are not necessarily easy to accept. It's difficult for a civilized person to accept an attack on long-held beliefs or notions. Without beating the point to death, I must warn you to leave the myths of civilization behind. Winter will not respect them, and they will not protect you. Recognizing our limitations and our humanity provides the key to enjoyment and survival. And it's most appropriate for our thinking to be restructured by lessons taken from the teachings of the Native American people, who knew camping and nature intimately.

Like the campers who have gone before you, you will find that winter camping is an inner experience as well as an outer one. The deep cold of a winter night is alien—and it can be fatal. It is also glorious. Like an astronaut in space, you will see the stars as you've never seen them. Looking up, you will feel the glory of it. That's when you know something is going on in your inner space. You can view the Center, where directions meet and life takes on a perspective and a depth unknown in civilized halls.

There is an irony involved. The more aware you are of winter's dangers, the safer you'll be. Knowing and respecting the danger involved will give you the wisdom to adjust and act prudently. The danger is livable as long as you let winter teach you about survival.

Survival lessons come without frills, and when you're winter camping, no passing entertainment will distract you from the basics of survival. Maybe it's a minor miracle that something as apparently simple as winter camping can teach so much. It exposes us to that which civilization and its traditions protects us from. Outside the confining protection of four walls, separated from society's lineal and sequential thought patterns, we come abruptly upon the difference between needs and wants. Needs are as solidly real as the demand for sound firewood. Needs are icicle-sharp, each one a standing exclamation mark on winter's ledger of survival requirements. If it does nothing else, winter will show us how few our true needs really are.

The philosophy drawn from winter camping encourages qualities like patience, perspective, humility, cooperation, reflection, and caution. These are hard to come by when you follow straight-line thought progressions, in which acceleration is constantly sought. Winter will never cooperate with hasty plans. When winter teaches, it bends our straight-line plans into a curve, then into a Hoop. When we are open to its lessons, winter shows us how to reach the balance needed to enjoy and benefit from our snowy outings.

Clothing

In the early 1970s when my interest in winter camping was revived, clothing was one of the first things I looked at. Clothing is the primary life-support system for winter activity, and I tried to find out more about it. I read historical records to see what Native Americans and early settlers had used. I looked at the kind of clothing used today by people who work outdoors and rely on good winter-wear in order to earn a living. I examined and tested "new" innovations, as well as items for camping and winter recreation. From this research I learned some basic facts about the following:

Layers. Clothing worn in layers is preferable to one heavy garment. Layering allows the individual to adjust clothing to activity level by adding or removing items as needed. Layers also help to reduce wind penetration or wind chill.

Durability. Winter is a rugged season, which calls for durable clothes. Things like zippers must be able to function at subzero temperatures, and in the case of zippers for winter use, an inner baffle is a *must*. The combination of attention to detail and quality consistent for winter use will give a durable winter garment.

Color. Dark clothing will pick up heat from the sun or fire, which reduces heat drain on the body. That is an important contribution under some conditions, but obviously not important if you're skiing hard and working up a sweat.

Wind Resistance. At least one garment in your kit should protect you from the wind. A tight, nylon shell jacket or over-pant will do. Heat loss when exposed to a strong or steady wind is considerable. A tight shell will, however, act as a vapor barrier, which may be a problem during times of heavy exertion.

Breathability. While working, the body must be able to shed moisture. For this, wool is one of the best choices, as are synthetics, which do not retain moisture. Loose layers of clothing allow moist air to be pumped out as you walk or ski. You don't want that vapor to stay with you by clinging to absorbent fibers. This is most critical with items worn near the skin, which explains the recent popularity of 'poly' undergarments.

You'll note that some of the categories do not complement one another. Wind resistance and breathability, for example, are at odds. Your final choices in clothing will need to reflect conditions you are apt to encounter and your planned forms of activity. Probably you'll find some clothing that will be fine while you're active and other clothes for use when you settle down at night.

Possibly the biggest danger is that of overdressing. It's best to shed clothing *before* you start to get heated up and sweaty. It doesn't take long to dampen a garment such as a vest. And, of course, a damp garment will not insulate as well when it's needed later. If you wait too long to shed you'll create problems for yourself.

While skiing I often wear only a loose wool jacket over my shirt and pants. It's floppy enough to pump out air and moisture as I move. While I'm on the go I can further cool myself by removing cap or mitts for a while. When I stop to rest, I add clothing as I cool down.

What I've described eliminates things like snowmobile suits or flight pants. Such items are not useful during times of exertion, and, in addition, they are bulky to pack along. It's possible to do without them for camping. They're warm and might be nice to have while sitting by the fire at night, but they take up a great deal of room in a pack and are very difficult to dry once they get damp.

The following describes clothing I use on winter trips. I've tried to make this information as useful as possible by pointing out compromises and alternatives. Quite likely you'll end up with different choices, but the basic considerations are the same.

Outer Clothing

Boots. Footwear is critical to comfort. Nothing endangers performance more than frosted extremities. Cold feet are not only painful, they can be dangerous and signal a too rapid loss of heat. The feet, being the farthest extremity, are the most difficult and therefore the most important part of the body to protect.

The warmest boots I ever used were called "bunny boots." They were made of felt and included a thick felt liner. Bunny boots were a military design and capable of taking military ski bindings. The army replaced these with an all-rubber boot with a sealed airspace. The rubber boots made your feet look like they'd been drawn by a cartoon artist, but they kept your feet warm.

Unfortunately, I don't have army supply lines to make using either of these boots practical. Once the felt gets wet a person is in for a lengthy process of drying it. When an air seal pops on the newer ones your insulation is gone with it. These items are good if you've an ample supply of spares.

Fortunately there is a simple, practical alternative to military boots. The solution is Arctic Pac boots, of which snowmobile boots are a version. Pacs have two common features. They have rubber bottoms and take removable felt liners.

Both features are important. Rubber bottoms allow one to move in slushy snow without getting damp. Also, when working around the fire in camp rubber bottoms keep the feet dry. Removable felt liners can, however, be taken out for drying if they do become damp. In addition, I always recommend carrying a spare set of liners as insurance.

Most pac boots come with leather uppers, but for camping I perfer nylon-topped snowmobile boots, which weigh less and are easier to pack. These work fine in camp and are equally suitable for use with snowshoes. An im-

portant feature of these boots is the drawstring top band, which closes and prevents snow from going down inside as you work in loose snow around camp. I keep my boots near the top of a pack so I can change into them as soon as the day's skiing is over.

A practical addition to pacs is a good inner sole that will insulate and protect the bottom of the foot. Most inner soles are made of felt, but I've cut my own from closed cell, or ensolite, foam. Closed cell foam doesn't crush, and retains excellent insulating qualities. As a bonus, it's not affected by moisture. But make sure your boot is roomy enough for liners and inner soles, because you don't want the boot pinching and retarding circulation.

A newer breed of boot is made with fixed liners of open cell foam and looks like boots used in outer space. These boots are a poor choice for camping, as the liners cannot be removed and open cell foam will hold water like the sponge it is. Open cell foam also crushes easily, and the more insulation crushes the less it insulates.

Most of my daytime travel is done on skis, so I wear ski boots. I prefer European touring styles with insulated uppers to be used with cable bindings. An overboot of wool adds insulation, and gaiters are essential for preventing loose snow from entering the boot to cause damp, easily chilled feet. Gaiters, incidently, will frost up inside and it's a good idea to clear them out from time to time. I unzip, remove, and shake mine vigorously to knock the frost away before it accumulates or melts.

Even the best-insulated and most waterproof ski boot is not warm. When you stop to rest or to have lunch you'll feel the cold creeping at your feet. Ski boots are not suitable for long stops—being warm requires that you be active. And, of course, being active causes the feet to sweat and act as heat sinks, which will dampen a boot from inside and out. The result? Words can't describe the sensation of slipping into frozen ski boots in the morning. It's the very last thing I do before leaving camp, and as soon as the boots are on I try to ski hard to warm myself and the boots up. You'll get used to it, but half-frozen footgear covered with frost will be "standard" after your first day.

Pants. I use heavy woolen pants held up with belt and suspenders. These are cut full (they look baggy), the legs are straight, and they are cuffless. The material in these is, I believe, called 30-ounce fabric. L.L. Bean and C.C. Filson handle superb woolen pants. I look for deep front pockets and rear pockets with button flaps.

Baggy trousers are not fashionable; they are functional. Even in a wind, your legs are protected by a zone of air trapped inside the trouser legs. A loose fit also allows for air circulation, which will dump excess heat and moisture while you work. It's a good way to stay amply protected without being overly insulated.

Shirt. A medium-weight wool or flannel shirt is my usual choice. The arms should fit loosely enought to allow for easy movement. Button flap pockets are a plus feature—you'll discover that when you've bent over, only to see something from your pocket fall into the snow and disappear. Once things hit the snow they are sometimes gone forever. If you like long, frustrating, frozen-fingered searches, then forget to button your pocket flaps. A good winter shirt will button at the neck to hold in heat, if needed, and will have an ample collar that can be turned up for wind protection.

Hat. My trademark is a trooper's hat made of rabbit fur. With ear flaps, neck protection, and a forehead cover, the trooper's hat is tops as winter headgear, especially when the wind is blowing. Unfortunately, the hat is too warm for use during periods of heavy exertion. For those times I use a lighter, woolen watch cap. My pack also contains a cap with a face mask for use if I must travel into a biting wind, or to wear while sleeping.

Wearing and removing the cap can be a means of helping regulate body temperature. But remove the cap before you become overheated, and replace it before you're chilled. Be especially cautious when it's windy, as one can quickly suffer frostbitten ears. If I'm in doubt about conditions, I keep my hat on and cool off by lowering my level of exertion.

Mitts. Leather mitts with removable wool liners are my first choice. They can be taken apart to be dried or changed. Spare liners for these are a must to include in your pack. Like your feet, the hands come into frequent contact with snow and cold. They are vulnerable, and protection is crucial. I have used mitts with cloth uppers that reach to the elbow. They are difficult to find, but they prevent snow from entering the mitts at the wrist. However, extra long mitts are far too warm to use while you're working hard. In selecting mitts and liners make sure they cover the wrist, an area of high heat loss.

I use boot oil on my mitt shells, and give them a complete going over to waterproof them. Oiled leather is colder, but it won't get soaked and frozen from coming into contact with snow and dampness. Non-oily waterproofing is somewhat better, but takes many applications for thorough sealing.

For skiing I keep a pair of light cotton gloves handy. These I use when working hard enough to make mitts too warm, but when it's still too cold or windy to ski barehanded. That's the only time I use gloves while winter camping. Otherwise, if you want warm hands, you need to wear mitts.

Vest. The vest is a useful item because it provides insulation for the body "core" or trunk. It can be worn under a light jacket or added to heavier clothes while you're inactive. Other times you can wear it by itself. It's a much-used piece of clothing on any trip.

The vest should have a stuff-sack so it will take up less room when you're not wearing it. Down stuffing works best as insulation, but there are good reasons to switch to synthetic fills. The problem with down is moisture. When down gets damp it loses much of its insulating property, and it is nearly impossible to dry on the trail. In most cases a vest can be removed before sweat dampens it, but if you're crossing a windy lake, for example, you may feel OK wearing the vest, only to find it's become visibly damp from your exertion. In comparison, good synthetic fills will retain insulating qualities even if wet. Synthetics don't stuff or pack as well, but they have other advantages.

Wool Jacket. During the day I wear a wool jacket that just covers the rear. The fit is loose so additional clothing can be worn under it. The looseness also helps moisture to escape as I move. It's a plus if the jacket has a wide collar that can be flipped up to provide wind protection. Unfortunately, that style of outdoor collar has fallen out of favor. Wool jackets from the Hudson Bay Company or C.C. Filson offer the features I like and they'll provide years of heavy use.

Down Jacket. The down jacket should have good "loft," which means it will look fluffy or inflated. The amount of loft indicates the amount of insulation in terms of trapped air. Other features should include zipper baffles, enough length to cover the rear, a throat cover or closure, drawstrings at bottom and waist, ample pockets, closed cuffs with full wrist coverage, and a hood that can be fitted to enclose the head. I prefer a detachable hood, which could be used in the sleeping bag if needed.

During the day, the down jacket is stuffed in a pack. When it's time to make camp I remove the jacket, shake it open, and allow it to "loft up" after being compressed all day. Especially in the cold, it takes some time for fibers to rebound and fluff up.

A good down jacket is costly, but treated wisely it will provide years of excellent service. It is just the thing when temperatures start to dip and you're inactive before turning in for the night.

Undergarments

Socks. In most cases I use two medium-weight socks instead of one heavy sock. However, what feels best to you is what counts. By all means, avoid getting too tight a fit that might restrict circulation or crush insulation around the foot.

Some people like to wear a very thin sock next to the skin and heavier woolen socks over that. Such layering is effective as long as your socks don't hold moisture near the foot. In the past, pure silk socks were available. They were used next to the skin because they didn't chafe or retain moisture.

Underwear Tops. I prefer two-piece underwear because it's easier to change. Either top or bottom can be removed without exposing the entire body to the cold.

Long-sleeved tops that fit close without binding work best for me. I've tried different styles and materials over the years. Bulky thermal knits are too warm for active use and they restrict movement. Ribbed knits and fishnet can chafe the skin. I've had the best results with Norwegian wool, ski-style underwear. It's light, soft, and allows the skin to breathe. A good fit is important, and proper washing and drying will help the fabric retain its shape. Some people object to wool, but the fabric keeps its insulating qualities even if it's damp, and that's important.

Underwear Bottoms. These are made of the same material as the tops. This wool layer is a second skin, so it should be comfortable and fit well. The fit should be firm without being tight. It's unwise to wear shorts or briefs under the wool because they trap moisture.

I carry an extra set of tops and bottoms on each trip. I view these spares as insurance that will give me a dry, fully insulating second skin in the event I get wet from an accident or overexertion.

Miscellaneous Items

Scarf. A scarf will protect the neck, but I've found them a bit of a nuisance in the bush. I'd substitute a dickey, easy to remove or put on. I find turtlenecks too warm if I'm active.

Handkerchief. Winter is hard on the eyes and nose. A large bandana handkerchief or two is standard equipment.

Glasses. Glare off the snow can be fierce. It's possible to severely strain the eyes, so I always carry ski goggles when I'm in the bush. I prefer goggles over sunglasses, as they provide protection if you're forced to travel into blowing snow.

That covers the clothing and accessories worn during the day. You may discover that some items are difficult to find and others are quite costly. My suggestions may even strike you as extreme or lavish. But keep in mind that ordinary winter clothing is not made for extended periods of outdoor use. It's made to look good or to get you from house to car or down the street. Study the topic of clothing carefully before you start making purchases.

In that regard you'll be exposed, as I am, to fantastic-sounding claims. Miracle fabrics, innovative designs, new products—where do these fit in? There's only one way to know for sure, and that's to try an item under actual conditions. I try to do that, and in so doing I have to admit there are some excellent new products. Hollow insulating fibers are excellent. Thinsulate by 3M is another new product that probably will be adapted for more and more winter uses. Synthetics that do not absorb moisture and that trap insulating air will have an impact that promotes recreational use.

Some of these miracles, however, will fall far short of the mark. I used wonder socks that were supposed to carry moisture quickly from the feet. I suppose they did so, but even in a clothes drier those socks took more than twice the time to dry as did ordinary woolen socks.

When I'm in doubt I tend to fall back on the known winners and old standbys. I know my woolen pants won't ice up at the bottom the way jeans or cotton pants will. I'm aware enough of function to make practical choices.

Items that have stood the test of time are usually the most reliable and functional.

Camping Equipment

Basic equipment for winter camping is similar to the gear used for summer camping. It is, however, more specialized for cold temperature use. The following is my equipment list and some discussion of the choice of gear:

Tent. I've been using the Eureka Timberline four-person tent—but for only two people. The extra room is a bonus for the additional gear needed in winter. The Timberline is easy to put up while wearing mitts, and it sheds snow well. In a heavy, wet snow the sides will begin to creep in, but a few light shakes will clear off any accumulation.

The Timberline has an optional vestibule, which can be attached to the front. This provides additional storage if it snows, and an area for using a stove during a storm. Eureka offers an "Expedition Model" of the Timberline, which comes with guy lines and a one-piece vestibule-fly. However, unless you're camping in an exposed, windy area, the regular Timberline will do fine. In fact, a wise winter camper will seek sites with natural wind protection for safety and comfort.

I'm quite sold on the Timberline for summer and winter use. It has quirks, to be sure, but it's a tent I can rely on. The Coleman Peak A-Frame is excellent, too, but lacks the option of a vestibule. Other quality A-frames that shed snow are available, but some are rather complex in terms of guy lines and small attachments that would require barehanded adjustments.

Cold is hard on tents. In some cases the urethane waterproofing will flake or crack where the wind flexes the frozen fabric. In other cases windblown snow will sandblast the coating off. Be on the alert for such damage and exercise more patience in erecting and folding your tent. The fabric will be stiff and slow to respond. Allow more time for fabric to adjust to any change in shape, especially where it must be folded over.

I put a six-by-eight-foot Versa Tarp under each Timberline. This prevents the tent from freezing to the ground and provides a clear area for set up and take down.

The best tent stake is a heavy metal spike with a welded arm. Plastic stakes will often shatter in the cold, and skewers will bend before they penetrate frozen ground. Most snow anchors require favorable snow conditions to work, so I rely on spikes. Mine are ten inches long, but I only drive in a few inches of the spike. In a short time it freezes in and is secure, and I've left enough of it exposed to twist and tap loose in the morning. Vivid paint or plastic ribbon will make your spikes visible in the event you drop one in the snow.

Fly. A ten-by-twelve-foot nylon fly is a good windbreak for use near the cooking area. To save time, I sometimes leave two parachute cords tied to the fly, which saves having to attach them with mitts removed. The cords, however, tangle easily, and it gets tricky if you have more than two to contend with when first setting up.

The Versa Tarp by Reef Industries is the only plastic tarp I know of that will take the cold. It's remarkable stuff; it will take years and years of use, as mine have. The clips furnished with the tarp are best attached indoors and left connected. An additional advantage of the Versa Tarp is that it has no coating to wear off. It can be buried in the snow to secure one edge and such freezing will not hurt it.

A fly is important for wind protection, as being exposed to the cold and wind drains away much energy. It's essential to have this kind of protection during severe weather. I don't leave a nylon fly up overnight, however. I drop it to the ground and put it aside so the wind won't be beating the brittle fabric all night.

Fire Building Tools. The basic tools are axe and saw. In some places the use of open fires is forbidden, but for winter camping in the Boundary Waters area, fire is practical and appropriate for both cooking and warmth. Each day of camping requires one tree for burning, and you must be sure to use dead, standing trees. Dead pines are easy to spot because they are bare of needles. Deciduous trees are dead when they show signs of loose bark falling away in large patches. I look for a tree that's about eight inches around where I'll cut it down.

Felling with the axe is easy in cold weather, and large chips will fly. The cold makes splitting wood easier, too. But first the tree must be dropped. When it's down, knock the limbs off with the axe, but be careful to set all branches aside to save for kindling and fuel. The bare trunk can then be cut into portable pieces with either axe or saw—using the saw wastes less wood. If you're on snowshoes or skis, a piece six to eight feet long can be dragged back to camp. Trips are made back and forth to carry the logs and branches to a spot near the cooking area. When the wood is in I like to stand inside the place cleared for cooking and saw off chunks of wood. The idea is to break the wood down to burning size as close to your cooking area as possible.

Getting the fire going can be difficult. The cold ground will pull heat from the fire, and as the ground thaws it will drown the lowest portion of the flame. It takes considerable heat to maintain a new fire, and it's often best to build one on several pieces of split wood. If it's windy the breeze will blow heat away from the fire faster than the fire can maintain itself. In that case, too, the flames will slowly die out. Such unfavorable conditions call for a solution—cheat. My cheating is done with kerosene or charcoal lighter. This is used prior to lighting the fire to "boost" the cold, new fuel. In the event of emergency, too, this would make it possible to produce a life-saving fire more quickly.

Stove. The Coleman Peak, one-burner stove will work in severe cold, but follow their instructions and recommendations carefully. I'd certainly practice lighting the stove outdoors in the cold at least a few times before departing. Once you get the hang of it you'll find the Peak a fine performer; it's lightweight and fuel efficient. I rely on wood for most of my cooking and heating, but there are times when the stove must fill the gap. In an emergency situation it can quickly be brought into use to prepare warm food or drink.

Cook Kit. Mirro's "Sierra" kit for four people is compact and useful. It has deep aluminum dishes that can be warmed by the fire before use. These dishes are perfect for serving soupy stews, which provide added liquid for campers, additional fluids being much needed for the rigors of winter. The coffeepot is small and not convenient for melting snow. However, another pail can be used for that. If your group is larger than four, use a regular Mirro camp cook kit.

I carry liquid soap to "soap" pots to be used over a wood fire and for cleaning up. The soap will freeze, but setting it close to the fire will melt enough for each use. Watch the bottle, though! It will melt if left too close to the flames.

Dishpan. In severe cold, plastic will shatter, so look for a pan made of aluminum or stainless steel. Winter cleanup is a chore that requires lots of warm water. A wood fire and ample pail will provide enough water for washing and rinsing.

Dispose of waste water away from camp. If food remains, try to burn it up. Snow cover makes finding disposal spots difficult. Eliminate from consideration any spot near water and confine disposal to rough-looking spots that won't be used by campers.

Shovels. For every two people I carry a small aluminum scoop shovel, similar to the kind carried in car trunks. Some have wooden handles, others plastic, still others are all aluminum, but the choice of material isn't as important as length. A longer handle means less bending over.

In areas of deep snow it is mandatory to remove the snow from each tent spot and the cooking area. Doing so is quite a bit of work. I've tried to avoid the effort by packing the snow down, but it never works when it's more than a foot deep. The reason is simple—older snow changes as winter progresses. The top layer is newer and often crusted. Below it the snow has become "corny" or "sugar snow." It is loose and defies packing. The small scoop shovel can cut the crust into pieces that can be tossed, and it will work fine for scooping up loose snow.

Candle Lantern. In cold weather, batteries lose most of their efficiency. It's not a good idea to count on a flashlight, so a candle lantern is my choice. There are two common styles. One style is spring loaded, but these are less desirable because the lantern is seldom warm enough for the spring to function as designed. Of the other styles that do not use spring-loaded candles I prefer those that take short, carafe candles. The traditional, or folding candle lantern, which looks like a small house, can be modified to take a carafe candle by making a holder from a large bottle cap.

When it's below zero a carafe candle will burn a long, long time. It's really quite efficient. There is always some danger when fire is used in a tent because it's easy to knock things over when moving about in close quarters, especially in winter. You must exercise caution.

Candle lanterns can be used outdoors, but the feeble winter flame is easily put out by the wind. For outdoor lighting, your campfire reflecting from the snowbanks will give ample light for most tasks. Any task requiring full light, however, should be done before dark, as neither campfire nor candle lantern will give off focussed or directed light.

Whisk Broom. During the night your tent will frost up inside. And, yes, it will do so even if the fabric is breathable. After packing my gear away I whisk down the walls to remove the frost, thus ensuring a drier tent at all times.

Thermos Bottle. A stainless steel insulated bottle full of hot, spiced tea sweetened with honey will help replace lost fluids and provide additional energy. Dry winter air places a demand on the body in that respect. I've made ensolite jackets for my bottles, and they keep things warm longer. Nothing will stay hot overnight, but it will at least stay warm.

Packs. I use the Duluth No. 3 Cruiser, which has a six-inch offset on each side. The slightly boxlike shape of these packs is ideal for the bulk of winter camping.

Travel Equipment

Travel in remote areas requires proper preparation, especially when the snow is deep and temperatures below zero. It is not just a matter of taking off into the wilderness. Travel conditions (the amount, kind, and condition of snow, for example) will change from one year to the next, or even during the course of a winter excursion. Going from deep, windless woods onto the hardpacked surface of a lake is typical of many trips. Each set of conditions presents different problems. The best way to prepare for your outing is to gain personal experience, ask questions in the local area, and devise a moderate, realistic plan.

My own experience has taught me to include both skis and snowshoes for a winter outing. Skis work well when the snow is firm, trails are wide and clear, and the terrain is not too rugged. On fresh snow; loose snow; winding, brushy trails; or difficult territory, snowshoes are a better choice. Often conditions change during a trip, as is the case when a damp snowstorm is followed by dry, cold weather. For this reason, an alternate means of transportation is essential.

Obviously, the problems encountered change with the number of people in your party. A small number is hard pressed to both break trail and move the equipment (it can be an overload for two campers faced with lots of fresh new snow). With larger numbers, some can rotate on breaking trail while others rotate on hauling equipment. Where a party may be forced to open or create trails, I'd want to have at least one person with a pair of snowshoes in my group.

But any group of winter campers should know something about travel equipment: what to look for and what works. There is more to cross-country skiing and snowshoeing that I can cover. The following basic considerations are, however, useful for planning a safe trip:

Skis. Cross-country touring skis are wider and heavier than racing or light-touring models. They can withstand heavier use, and the wider ski will give more support (flotation) on trails. Skis are not particularly handy for use on winding or brushy trails. In addition, wilderness trails often include obstacles that are hard on skis (rocks, fallen logs, and holes). If your entire trip will be in tight, wooded country then I'd not include skis. But if you'll be spending time crossing frozen lakes or on wide trails, then skis are excellent. In any case, a ski for use in a wilderness setting should be sturdier than one intended for use on groomed trails.

The next concern is bindings. I use cable bindings because they are strong and able to take the strain and heavy use of breaking trail and pulling equipment. When I mount cable bindings, I always inject epoxy into the screw holes. It is important to have a secure binding capable of holding up under days of winter travel.

Pin bindings have all but replaced cable bindings on most skis. If you were to be free-skiing and not hauling equipment, then probably pin bindings would be sufficient. Still, I feel better with heavier skis and cable bindings because I know they'll not only take the heavy use, but they'll also take the abuse handed out by ski-eating trails. In addition, I like the heavier boot used with a substantial cable binding, because it gives more foot protection. If you've never used cables, some practice will give you a feel for them.

Over the years I've used a wide variety of skiing equipment. That includes everything from light racing skis to mountaineering skis with cable bindings that lock for downhill runs. The conventional touring ski, which I use most often, falls somewhere in the middle. If I were facing a trip into a new environment, I'd consider renting skis, with the idea that equipment rented locally would be better adapted to local conditions. But even at home I've sometimes rented equipment in order to cope with the environment. For example, I've used rental no-wax skis in late fall and spring when snow conditions vary wildly from sun to shade, creating slow slush one minute and an iced runway the next.

Most of the winter, however, I do nicely on skis that require waxing. I find that they move more easily than no-wax models. After redoing the pine tar bottoms, I use a cold temperature, hard wax on the entire bottom. This gives me a fast ski with suitable glide, and it will work for most mid-winter days when the conditions are consistently cold and dry. The area under the foot is where I wax and change waxes to provide kick. This is an easy system to live with and makes altering wax on the trail a relatively simple procedure. (It takes me a few minutes, but I've had lots of practice.) A small wax kit containing suitable waxes, scraper, and cork should be included with your equipment. Carry it where it will be handy. In mine I'm also sure to include at least one spare ski tip to repair a ski that runs afoul of a wilderness trail.

I remember when ski poles were bamboo rods with round baskets on the ends. That is, of course, the basic form of any pole, but the ones today are designed for faster running, with baskets that avoid snagging. But even these will catch if you're on a brush-choked trail. When that's the case, your pace will be slowed. Deep snow will slow you, too. For that condition it's nice to have an oversized basket, which will give more push. I've made oversized plastic disks that tie to my baskets. When not needed, the disks can be removed and kept with the wax kit. I know a number of people, too, who use ski poles with their snowshoes. I don't do it myself, but it's something you may wish to experiment with.

Snowshoes. I prefer a snowshoe with a sharp upturn at the toe and a fairly long tail. Alaska or Pickrel models fit such a design. The upturned front helps to avoid hooking the toe in crusted snow. The long tail makes the shoe heavier at the rear, which means the toe webbing will always rise higher than the foot, thus clearing the way. This is excellent for breaking trail. A snowshoe that doesn't drag at the tail will have to be lifted higher with each step, requiring extra effort.

Folk wisdom advises us to use a snowshoe like the Bear Paw for brushy country. Unfortunately, *nothing* works well in thick alder brush, and I suspect the round, flat, Bear Paw design was developed for use on pack snow. For performance on established trails or for flotation on fresh snow, the Alaska or Pickrel will do the job.

It is important to get a snowshoe large enough for your weight. I weigh about 155 pounds, and I use a snowshoe fifty inches long by ten inches wide. A common error is buying a shoe that is too small, as people assume a smaller shoe will be easier to handle. Not so. Too small a shoe will simply sink farther. (In fresh snow, even a big shoe will often sink a foot or more when you're making trail.) The person breaking trail is literally climbing straight up, so the less sinking the better.

I get my wooden snowshoes in Canada, and I look for a good price. Name brand shoes are excellent, but they'll break as easily as generic shoes when a person gets hung in a hidden obstruction or accidentally bridges a shoe between two high spots.

For bindings I've come to rely on the Type H in leather. They've given me years of good service. The Type H is available in neoprene and nylon, but those tend to fray and gather ice on the loose threads.

Snowshoes and bindings can build up ice coatings, but this tends to happen only when you're crossing water and encounter slush. It can become a dangerous condition as your shoes grow larger and heavier. Wooden and plastic shoes with webbings of leather or synthetic cord will be less prone to ice up. Metal snowshoes and metal bindings for mountain use will ice readily—I'd reserve them for high, dry country.

I use snowmobile boots when snowshoeing. After going a short distance it is usually necessary to stop and tighten the binding. However, the binding will stay once it adjusts to the boot. With new bindings it may take a day or more for things to work in. The heel of your boot should be able to move from side to side by five inches. More than that, your binding is too loose.

Snowshoes are awkward at first. Beginning showshoers fall frequently, usually after one shoe overlaps the other. Having fallen, the novice tries walking bowlegged—discovering new dimensions of pain. But the trick to snowshoeing is simpler than that and doesn't hurt at all. Maintain a stride that keeps one foot in front of the other; even when standing, one foot should stay well in front. This allows the shoes, which are tapered, to clear one another. When walking, I try to place the foot that is moving forward slightly ahead of the toe of the other snowshoe. This makes my stride close to two feet long, but aside from long steps, this gait is fairly natural. As I move forward, I give each shoe a slight flick to the outside, which adds a little clearance and shakes off accumulated snow.

Snowshoeing is slow and strenuous when you have to make trail. The energy demands are enormous. But, given identical conditions of deep new snow, I'd rather plow along on snowshoes than be knee deep and struggling on skis.

The Towing-Toboggan

You must have noticed by now. I'm placing a great deal of emphasis on being well prepared for deep cold, weather changes, and other contingencies. A prudent winter plan must be more than minimal in what it includes. Yet, there is a problem. How does one move all that extra equipment? Even though not much heavier than summer gear, the insulating clothes and other articles of winter are bulkier. How does one manage?

I manage the transition from summer camping by replacing my canoe with a towing-toboggan. The toboggan allows me to take what I need without being restricted to what will conveniently fit on my back. I find it easier, too, towing the weight rather than carrying it. This makes both skiing and snowshoeing easier, at least part of the time. When backpacking your gear there's seldom a break, but with towing it's possible to trade off and enjoy some variety. The task of travel is improved and you have an extra margin of safety by being amply supplied.

People look at the towing-toboggan and they think, "That looks like *work*!" It is work, but it's manageable. An eight-foot toboggan will serve four people, and each of the four would tow for twenty minutes once every eighty minutes. That's not so bad, and quite typical for smooth-going across lakes. But even in hilly country or when breaking trail there's a chance for some relief as people "spell" one another or use teamwork to negotiate a tough spot.

I'm convinced that towing provides the best option. Independent backpacking has too many physical limitations and lacks the variety available in towing.

The rig I'm going to describe can be built at home for a modest cost. The main items are the toboggan and a pack frame. It's likely you already have either or both of these. If so you have ninety percent of the project. The rest is in the form of small items easily secured at a hardware store or lumberyard. Some varieties of the towing-toboggan can be purchased, however. These are often called "pulks." They tend to be smaller and are intended to carry the gear of one or maybe two people.

As the towing rig is described you'll find illustrations along the way. I think most of it will be clear enough, but if you're in doubt check both text and illustrations for guidance.

The first item is a pack frame with hip belt. The bottom portion of the frame, near the hip belt, becomes the anchor point for the towing poles. The frame is not harmed by the addition of two quarter-inch, open hooks for attaching the poles. On the trail, this pack is used to carry clothing removed during times of exertion. The pack should not be loaded with weight, which makes the work harder. Towing is hot work—it's best if the frame has a ventilated back.

Next come the towing poles, which hook onto the pack frame. On my rig these remain fixed to the toboggan, but they could be made to lift off there, too. The poles pull the load and also prevent it from running you over on a downhill. As you start downhill you'll feel the load nudge into you before it settles into position. Be ready to snowplow and anticipate turns if you're on skis.

The poles are made from stock lengths of three-quarter-inch conduit (sometimes called EMT), which comes ten feet long. Through trial and error I've come to prefer poles at least eight feet long. Cable loops fixed to the end of each pole give the simplest form of U-joint. They allow the rig to turn and flow over bumps with ease.

An illustration shows the end of a pole that has been flattened and trimmed to eliminate sharp corners. The cable loop is held in place with an eighth-inch cable clamp, which simply bolts through the flattened conduit. Plastic-coated cable (commonly used on garage doors) works best. I've never had a cable loop jump off the open hook on the pack frame, but it could happen, especially on a downhill run.

The toboggan does not need to be changed much; it takes additions. Hooks or U-bolts at the front bow are used to attach the towing poles. Side rails are formed of half-inch conduit, which is joined to a conduit loop formed at the back of the toboggan. Conduit pieces are bolted in place; I wouldn't trust wood screws for the job. Canvas sides help to hold the packs in. The canvas is secured to the conduit and to the grab rope that runs along the side of the toboggan.

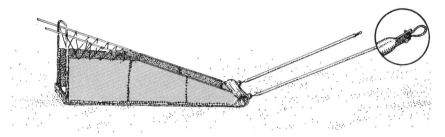

As the illustration shows, the towing toboggan looks a little like a dog sled. What you'll have to do in order to attach the towing poles, conduit frame, and the rest, will depend on how your toboggan is constructed. Your finished product should be sturdy and capable of some flex.

An important addition is the keel, located at the rear-center. The keel on mine is a piece of one-inch angle aluminum that has been beveled and sharpened. It's bolted in place with counter-sunk bolts. My keel is eight inches long. On packed snow the keel keeps the tail of the toboggan from swinging side-to-side. A toboggan that tracks well wastes less energy in towing. A sharp bevel on the keel helps the toboggan ride over buried branches without wrenching the back of the person doing the towing.

Most measurements will have to suit the size of toboggan you're working with. But I want to point out a feature you should try to include. The side rails extend past the rear loop by eight inches. Those eight-inch extensions serve as short handles, and they also provide a place where you can mount a detachable push-bar.

The push-bar is made of three-quarter-inch conduit bent in a U to fit over the protruding side rails. A full length of conduit bent in a U gives an extension at the rear of more than four feet. It is held in place by drilling holes through the bar and side rail extensions and then dropping a pin in place. My pins have a cord tied to them to avoid loss, but it's still good to have a spare.

The push-bar extends back far enough so a person on skis or snowshoes can push. The bar can also be used to lift and turn the rear on tight bends. Climbing steep inclines or getting through brushy trails is easier with one pulling and another pushing. When not needed, the push-bar can be stowed with the load.

There are a few other things that complete the rig. The bottom of the toboggan should be waxed with paraffin so it will slide easily. In crusty snow your wax will wear off quickly, so carry extra wax for the job.

I tie a small sack of spare parts to the rig. This contains screwdriver, pliers, wrench, cable pieces, cable clamps, and a few bolts and screws suitable for toboggan or ski-binding repairs.

The passenger area of a toboggan has cleats every foot or so. Between these cleats, I place pieces of two-inch thick styrofoam for seating in the evening. It sure beats sitting on a frozen log. Spray paint these a visible color that will stand out against the snow. There should be one "seat" for each person.

My toboggan rig is basic and sound. It looks improvised, but the finished product is functional for moving camping gear in winter. I've tried variations, such as using a small plastic toboggan for each person, however, I much prefer the larger wooden toboggan as described. An eight-foot toboggan will handle the gear for four people. You *could* use an eight-foot toboggan for six people, but I think the workload is more manageable when three or four people share a toboggan and use teamwork.

When loading the toboggan put the heaviest packs at the rear. Keep the front light, so it will ride up on the snow and help pack it down ahead of the weight. In deep, fresh snow you don't want the toboggan pushing a wave of snow in front of itself. When that happens it's best to put more effort into breaking trail before the toboggan. With larger groups, two people on snowshoes can be sent ahead to lay down a trail for the rest to follow. But remember to set up a timetable for rotating jobs—those opening the trail and those towing will need rests. For smaller parties, breaking trail and towing will keep everyone busy and working heavily. Frequent breaks will be needed to rest and drink.

Travel Technique

Winter camping virtually hinges on being able to travel. Part of the experience comes from journeying through the almost alien beauty of winter landscapes. But safe and practical travel requires good judgment and a variety of skills, which can be sharpened only through experience. A few good days can lull a person into being overconfident. With that in mind, the following discussion of travel technique is provided for perspective:

Skiing. Of late, cross-country skiing has been a major contributor to renewed interest in winter activity, including camping. Skiing is appealing, and it provides a reliable form of transportation. There are, however, limitations.

For the most part, cross-country skiing will work where there are established, used trails; when there is a thick crust on the snow (most often in February and March); and on lakes where snow has been packed by the wind. All of these conditions provide relatively easy skiing. Lake skiing, in particular, is level and provides good going, though a strong wind coming across five miles of frozen lake is a factor to be reckoned with.

It is helpful to avoid too much exposure to the wind. The chilling effect of wind on a sweating body is tremendous, and it can cut into your energy reserves in no time. It's best to stay out of the wind when possible. Islands and points will give some shelter while you travel, and staying close to shore will enable you to take shelter in a bay.

Winter travel on lakes requires attention to ice conditions. Ice is usually safe by late December. However, during winters when we have heavy snow the ice will sink under the snow-pack, creating slush. In that case, the members of your party must fan out. Following a fresh track will cause skis to ice up in just a few minutes. Your tracks will usually freeze overnight and can be used the next day. Most of the time it works to follow an existing trail, but if it is snowcovered, it may turn slushy.

Areas around inlets and outlets on lakes are potentially dangerous. Moving water weakens ice, and such areas should be given a wide berth. Even a light snow cover will hide danger spots, so be wary. Weak spots or ice that's starting to thaw will look darker. But, again, snow cover may hide that.

River travel is even more risky. Unless you know the river intimately (including freezing patterns and the location of rapids, rocks, and channels) it is best to stay off. Like lake ice, river ice will sink under a heavy snow load, and even a languidly flowing river can cause dangerously thin ice under the snow. For my part I do not travel on frozen rivers; I follow the crest of the riverbank for a safe route.

Cross-country skiing in the bush tends to be most appropriate for the open spaces where one can speed along. Frequently used trails or well-packed snow bases are the ideal medium for cross-country skiing. When conditions favor skiing you'll have what I feel is the best way to enjoy the winter wilderness.

While enjoying it, you'll also be learning new things. If your skiing lacks a strong "kick," a few turns at the towing toboggan will correct that. A vigorous kick is essential when you tow the toboggan. How you use your body weight is also important. Always lean forward to start the toboggan or move it over a rise.

A moderate skiing pace is wise. A group of four, towing a toboggan and stopping for normal rest periods, will average about two and a half miles per hour. It is strenuous work, so it is best to take advantage of the natural glide of skis. The glide is rest time, and after a while you learn how to use that to advantage. A safe pace is one that can be maintained without overheating. The work of towing will make you feel damp, but you do not want to get soaked by sweat. Try for a strong kick followed by a forward-leaning glide. It is definitely a much slower technique than that used free skiing.

Showshoeing. In comparison to skiing, snowshoeing is a plodding affair. Because there is no glide in snowshoeing, the overall exertion is greater mile-for-mile. However, snowshoeing *will* get you there, and it will work in conditions that make skiing either impractical or impossible.

The long, flicking stride of snowshoeing is hard on leg muscles. There is a lot of stretching involved. It's best to go easy, or travel the next day will be hampered by stiff muscles. It is difficult to condition yourself for snowshoeing, because anything less than working through deep snow is too much like walking.

Snowshoes can break if you trip on covered branches, hook a toe on the snow crust, bridge the shoe between two firm places, or come down hard on a stump or other hazard. In many cases, a cracked frame can be bound together with nylon cord, an emergency repair that will last the duration of a trip if care is used.

Steep rises and drops present special problems. The toe of the shoe extends forward enough to prevent climbing. In that case, it may be necessary to sidestep up a slope. It's neither graceful nor easy, but it will work. On moderate slopes, dig in the toe of your boot to keep from slipping back. Snowshoes are designed to do that, so your toe should be able to poke through the large hole on the centerline of the shoe. If it doesn't, your rigging is wrong.

Going downhill is tricky, too. Snowshoes will ski down a steep slope, and there's little that can be done to control them. Snowshoes make impossible skis, because the shoe itself holds the foot in a position that forces the body to lean (fall, really) downhill. Sidestepping down a hill may be your only choice.

Trails. Whether on skis or snowshoes, it is best to follow an existing trail. Even an old trail provides some base; much better than wading through trackless snow. A trail will often remain soft the day it is made, but it becomes firm by the following day. Once trails are opened and used,

travel is easier, safer, and faster.

If you are breaking or reopening a trail, two people on snowshoes can put down a good path. As stated earlier, the rest of the group can follow on skis, but there is an obvious conflict in the making. The trail breakers will be worn out if they are forced to stay out front for too long. Fair distribution of the workload is essential.

In a party of six people it is best to have two or three sets of snowshoes and six sets of skis. Three snowshoers can rotate the lead for an hour; then they can switch to skis and let the other three open the trail. This arrangement provides reasonable rotation. Your total rate of travel will be slow, about one mile per hour, but that's darn good considering the conditions.

Once you have a trail, your return trip can be done on skis in half the time, or less. That is, if it doesn't snow in the meantime. In planning daily travel assume you'll move at slow speed. Five or six miles of fresh trail work is plenty to accomplish during the limited daylight of winter.

Rest Periods. The exertion of opening trails, towing, and being in a cold environment is enormous. Even a rest break in the cold takes far more energy than resting during warm weather. However, rest periods are important.

Rest periods, like intervals in training, allow the body to rebound. While at ease, heat can dissipate, the heart can stabilize, and damp clothing can dry somewhat. Often, I take off my jacket and shake it in the cold dry air to get moisture out of it, while at the same time allowing excess heat and moisture to leave my trunk.

The traveler should constantly be aware of the need to replenish fluids to offset loss due to exertion in dry air. The thermos bottle should be kept at hand. Dehydration reduces body efficiency; it even upsets mental processes. Eating snow or sucking ice won't curb the feeling of thirst. To a limited degree, it reduces body temperature, but it should not be done too often. Our mouths can't take much severe cold without damage to gums and soft tissue. Besides, it takes more than a dozen cups of snow to equal one cup of water.

Rest breaks also allow time for high-energy food or snacks. Something to munch on will begin helping the system in about a half hour. The reaction to sugars is faster. Snacking along the way simply recognizes the energy requirements of being outdoors doing heavy work.

Take a brief or "standing" rest every twenty minutes—when people rotate places on the trail. A longer rest should follow every sixty minutes of travel.

Lunch should be long enough for a good rest, but not long enough to get chilled. It's best to stop in a protected place, because a steady wind can turn a lunch break into torture. Usually, I carry frozen sandwiches for lunch. Frozen sandwiches are not a gourmet item, but under the circumstances they are convenient, edible, and will keep all winter. If possible, heat water by melting snow or ice, and try to keep the thermos filled.

Luckily, winter trails are rewarding. Travel is not all drudgery, caution, and frozen food. A trail will usually pass through many different animal habitats, each one with its own beauty and characteristics. Animal tracks in the snow and birds flitting in the trees are part of the picture. The moderate pace I've described will provide time to see and enjoy these things, which is part of the reason for being there.

Making Camp

In the north country, winter brings a shortage of daylight. In December and January, there are about eight hours of day, with darkness starting around 4:00 in the afternoon. As soon as the sun goes down, temperatures begin to plunge.

For winter campers, half of the day is devoted to travel. Over that four hours, you will cover from five to ten miles, depending on conditions and method of travel. That same distance could be covered in half the time if you were free skiing, but it's plenty when trails need opening and you're towing a load.

By 2:00 in the afternoon you should be ready to set up camp. That allows only two hours of light for the entire process, and you may end up finishing your meal in the dark. Everything takes more time in the winter.

It's important to get camp set up while the light and temperature are in your favor. Setting up camp is an even slower process if you start too late. It's a hassle to stumble around in the twilight while the cold settles in and you would rather be sitting down to eat. If you are faced with a choice of making camp on time in a "poor" location or pushing on for another hour to reach a "better" spot, make the best of the poor location.

The first task in making camp is to clear off an area for tents and cooking. On most campsites the cleared areas are obvious. If you are at an undeveloped site, it may take more time to search out decent tent spots.

The idea of digging away the snow surprises many people. I'm often asked, "Don't you just pack the snow down?" The answer is no. In the first place it would take tremendous amounts of packing to flatten four feet of snow into something solid and stable. It's easier to shovel it away. Second, snow in the north is usually dry and granular, like sand. It doesn't pack well unless you mix upper and lower layers of snow and allow them to set for a period of time. Besides, your fire would end up in a deep, awkward hole if you tried to work on top of the snow.

Shoveling gives an easy-to-use camp spot, but it's a big job when the snow stands hip deep as you start. With two people working it will take nearly an hour to clear off a tent and cooking area. But it's time well spent because the result is a sheltered depression where you can camp and cook in relative comfort.

It is most convenient when the tents face the cooking area. They should not, however, be too close to the fire, because sparks can burn holes in a tent. It's better to have too much distance than too little.

The space you dig for the tent must be wide enough so you can work around the tent. The area should be dug out extra long if you plan to use a vestibule. While shoveling you may uncover some obstructions. Most logs can be broken free and moved. Huge logs or rocks may force you to shift your digging or even force you to move to another location. Minor holes can be leveled using snow, but avoid having too deep a snow pad, as it can settle and cause other problems.

Remember that you will be working in a hole. Putting up the tent must be thought out in advance. The work space is limited, and complex tents often require more than minimal space. The Eureka Timberline is, however, self-supporting and can be erected and shifted in close quarters. Once your tent is in position it can be secured with the kind of spikes I described earlier. As an alternative you could use a log or crossed sticks for a snow anchor.

When the tent is up and secured, put your personal gear inside where it will be out of the way. Skis, snowshoes, poles, firewood, and other outdoor items go along the shelf formed by your excavation. They will be at eye level and out from under foot—very important with the limited space you'll have. Small items that would be buried if it snowed during the night should be stored under cover, before dark if possible.

The cooking area comes next. It is formed as a continuation of the area excavated for tents. The best plan places the cooking fire in a corner. That way, both heat and light are reflected toward people by the white snowbanks. The cooking area should be made large enough for the entire group to sit around.

Designated campsites in wilderness areas have a fire grate. You're supposed to use it. But even if you could find the grate under the snow, it is still best to build your fire immediately in front of it. A grate is too low and inconvenient for tending a winter fire.

To get a fire going, I use small wood (twigs, split kindling, dry bark, and shavings) to begin building a base of heat. Later, I place a log up to eight inches in diameter on either side of the fire. These big logs contain the heat before they start burning themselves. A new fire will require much tending and frequent fueling with small wood. Your fire must be well established before cooking starts. The ground must have a chance to heat, otherwise the fire will fizzle out (literally freeze out). When you are ready to cook, a stainless steel backpacker's grid will span the two logs to give you a stable cooking area.

If your fire is built in a corner close to the bank, poke long sticks into the snowbank and hang pots over them. A tag alder pole five or six feet long works well for this. (Cutting birch, maple, or other valuable trees is not recommended. Alder, however, is brush that won't be missed. You could carry conduit pieces to substitute for wood poles if you'd rather not get involved with selective cutting of brush.) Plunge at least four feet of the pole into the snowbank above the fire. Leave the thicker butt end sticking out, as it will take the weight of a full pot. After cooking, these poles can be used to hold mitt liners and other equipment or clothing near the fire for drying. Keep an eye on anything left to dry. Many a sock has been "toasted" because it was left unattended.

Now let's try to imagine what this kind of camp looks like. You are in a hole. Walls of snow about four feet high surround you. Your fire is reflecting heat and light into your work area. If you sit down on your foam block from the toboggan, the wind will pass over your head. The snowbank near the fire is slushy, and it provides a ready source of snow for melting. Keep a pot hanging over the fire and you've a source of water conveniently at your side. Heat, light, wind protection, and water are all provided. It takes more effort to establish this sort of camp, but it has obvious benefits.

The only other thing you may need is a ramp or steps cut in the snowbank so you can get in and out of the hole easier. This is particularly helpful when the snow is four feet or more in depth.

The kind of site I've described works even better if it has natural protection from trees. One of the best spots I ever found was a small clearing in the center of a stand of balsam fir. The wind was nil, and when it snowed we didn't get drifted in. A protected site is an asset. In contrast, most summer sites are "scenic"—they have a view, which means they are open to the wind. If you must camp on such a site, provide as much cover as possible and at least move to the edge of the tree line.

At this time, winter campsites are not common. Winter camping has not caught on enough for state and federal agencies to develop sites specifically for winter use. The time for that may come. In particular, designated winter sites would have the benefit of established, used trails. Also, the problem of waste disposal could be better addressed. In winter, digging is nearly impossible and disposal of human and food wastes needs a better solution than surface disposal.

As you plan your trip, be sure to check with the agency charged with managing the land where you'll be camping. In designated wilderness areas, travel permits are often required. It also makes sense to let someone in the area know where you will be in case you become lost or snowed in. This helps to narrow the search—a vital factor. Likewise, it is absolutely necessary that at least one person back home be given your exact plan and route to be passed to searchers if needed.

Beyond what I have mentioned, there are few formal restraints on winter camping. Cooperation with land management agencies is good common sense. Cooperation will allow managers to begin planning for winter users, and winter campers can make their needs known. Such effort will be a major contribution toward good quality winter camping in the future.

Sleeping

Getting a good night's rest is essential if you are to perform well and enjoy the coming day. All camping is like a stool with three legs. The legs are: Eat Well, Sleep Well, Stay Warm and Dry. Those three legs support all camping trips, no matter how humble or grand. For a winter trip, the basics of camping are vital.

I once made the mistake of telling an interested person that I "slept cold" while winter camping. The look on the person's face was full of confusion and pity. Quickly, I explained that my comment meant that I don't try to heat a tent in winter. I rely on my sleeping equipment to insulate and hold my body heat.

However, the topic of heating tents is important. It's something I don't do because it is dangerous. With bulky clothing and bed rolls it is just too easy to bump into a stove. Nylon tent floors become extremely slippery in the cold, and it is hard not to slide around. The fire danger is real, and you would have to be alert all night to prevent resting against an exposed stove surface. There is an additional danger from fumes. Even a breathable tent can and will frost up, becoming airtight and trapping dangerous gasses inside. The weight of fuel and stoves is another consideration.

Winter camping used to be done in heated tents. Those were canvas tents with a stovepipe adaptor for a tiny wood stove. A canvas tent can take some heat; nylon can not. Tents designed or intended to take stoves tend to be large, heavy-walled tents, not the sort of thing to be moved with ease.

Relatively portable winter camping will eliminate heating stoves in favor of more insulation. Following is a detailed account of what is needed, what to consider, and what to do:

Sleeping Equipment

Foam Pads. The ground under the tent is frozen, and it will drain heat from the body if you are not adequately insulated. Foam sleeping pads come in two types. These are (1) open cell foam and (2) closed cell foam (ensolite). Of the two, closed cell pads are *far* more effective. In addition, closed cell comes in two varieties—summer and winter. The winter variety is more flexible in the cold, however, even it gets stiff when the temperature is below zero. You have to lay on the pad for a while to let it warm and slowly flatten.

Good pads tend to be quite firm because they hold small trapped pockets of dead air. Any pad that will compress greatly won't hold as much insulating air. Likewise, an air mattress won't do for winter, because it holds a single mass of air. Insulation depends on tiny capsules of noncirculating air. For this reason, two inches of open cell foam won't do as good a job as a three-eighths-inch pad of closed cell.

Sleeping pads commonly come twenty inches wide by forty inches long. Those dimensions are suitable to cushion hips and shoulders for summer camping. For winter use, three such pads become the sleeping platform for two people. Two pads go side-by-side and one goes across the top or bottom. This sleeping platform may be too "cozy" for some people, but sleeping that close does reduce heat loss. The pads will sometimes slide apart, and you may have to reposition them during the night. You'll know shortly when a hip, heel, or elbow rests on the frigid ground.

Sleeping Bags. My first winter bag was a Woods sleeping robe, made in Canada. It came in a large duffel twice the size of a modern winter bag. My next winter bag was a Black's Icelandic Special, a third smaller than the Wood's robe.

Those bags were of top quality down, had a full cut, and were very expensive. In those days, goose down was the premier filler and insulation. I'll admit that down packs (stuffs) well, but it has serious drawbacks. Down does not dry easily and tends to stay damp, consequently losing much of its insulating properties. Additionally, though down will fluff or "loft" into a thick insulating layer above, the down under a sleeper will be crushed to nothing and provide minimal insulation.

Today's sleeping bags are cut differently and often use newer insulating fills to do the same job with half the bulk needed when I was a youth. I'd not advise that you buy a special winter bag unless you intend to do a lot of winter camping, though. The use of such bags is limited to severe cold. However, if you study good winter bags, you can get some ideas for putting together an adequate package for sleeping in winter.

It takes a minimum of four pounds of insulation fill, or roughly six inches of "loft," for below-zero camping. Synthetic fills (Hollofill, Polar Gard, Fiberfill II) don't loft as well as down, but they don't crush underneath as much. That's a reasonable trade. Synthetic fills will also insulate if they are damp—an impossible task for down.

If you put one summer bag inside another, you can create winter protection without the expense of a specialized bag. But if you use two bags, make sure they are not too tight. They must be able to loft up. Some manufacturers offer this option as part of their sleeping bag series. Properly done, the two-bag system works well in winter, is affordable, and offers the option of year-round use.

People have asked me about zipping bags together so two campers can sleep together. The warmth shared by two bodies would be nice, but it is difficult to control heat loss from the top of the bag. I suspect the shoulders would be too exposed.

Of course, you see the solution to *that* little problem. Why don't our two campers snuggle up and cover their heads with the combined sleeping bags? A good idea, except for the amount of moisture it would put inside the bags. On a one-or two-night trip it might not make any difference, but it's not a good idea to breathe into your sleeping bag, causing it to get damp and insulate less effectively.

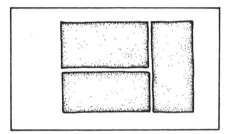 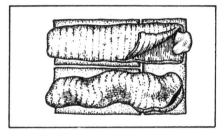

Sleepwear. In cold weather, a bare body is unable to heat up an entire bag enough for comfortable sleep. A zone of warm air must be held close to the body. As you relax and doze off, your body temperature drops. The sleeping bag and foam pad slow down heat loss, but the first line of defense is right next to the skin.

In moderate winter temperatures, a set of clean, dry long underwear will hold heat next to the body. In colder temperatures, the underwear should be replaced by quilted, insulated tops and bottoms. In severe cold, both long underwear and insulated tops and bottoms must be worn. These combinations extend your sleeping comfort over a wide temperature range. It's important not to overdress. You don't want to get sweaty. For convenience, all that underwear can go inside the bag with you. Then you can remove or add pieces during the night as needed.

Note, too, that the extra underwear and quilted tops and bottoms also provide emergency clothing if you or someone in your party need a change of clothes.

If you have been sweating during the day, it is best to change out of the clothes you were wearing. Get down to the skin and put on separate clothes for sleeping. Do not put wet or damp clothing in the sleeping bag. Your clothes will be ice cold when you put them on in the morning, but they will warm up once you put them on. That includes things like boots. I've had people tell me that a sleeping bag can be used to dry damp clothes and frozen boots. Nonsense. What that does is reduce the efficiency of your sleeping bag while doing very little either to warm or dry your clothing. It sounds good, but getting out of a nice warm sleeping bag is a shock, no matter how you try to sneak up on it.

Socks, mitts, wool cap, and face masks can also be worn in the sleeping bag. Those things, too, should be dry. If you continue to feel cold, put on your vest, parka hood, or coat. I recall two nights in a row when I slept with my entire parka on; I understand it got down to -37°F both times.

Before I lie down for the night, I spread my wool jacket over the foot of my sleeping bag, which seems to slow heat loss. A light woolen blanket or flannel sheet can be used to cover both sleeping bags, if you have room to carry it. It will hold back some heat, and it will catch the frost that forms from breathing. That's important. As much as possible you want your breath and its moisture directed away from the sleeping bag, certainly not into it. If your face feels too cold use a face mask.

Winter nights are long. It's not unusual to spend ten or more hours in the sleeping bag. When you wake up, you will still feel tired. After all, your body has been working all night to stay warm. The feeling of tiredness means your body requires fuel. Dried fruit or candy will perk you up; I often munch on something when I awake. You'll also feel very thirsty. Dry, cold air leaves a person feeling parched. I've had limited results keeping liquids warm overnight. It would be nice to get up to a hot cup of sweet tea, but most often my thirst must wait until more snow can be melted over a fire.

Once you are up, brush frost off bags and check them for damp spots. The cold, dry air will dry a bag somewhat if you spread and shake it. However, when you are surrounded by snow it is hard to keep things perfectly dry. Nearly everything you touch or bump can turn to water, so cautious airing and drying is best. Be very aware of the roof, which can send down a shower of frost if you brush against it. Your sleeping pads will roll up easier if they are still warm from sleeping on them. It's best to roll up and stuff away the bigger items promptly upon arising.

Little details are important to a night's rest. The right equipment or right combinations will allow you to adapt to a variety of conditons. It's tempting to lighten the load and eliminate some of what I've described, but don't do so too hastily. In the extremes of weather you will need everything mentioned here.

Food and Menus

The body's fuel is food. When you are exposed to the elements, food generates the heat needed to keep you warm. The winter camper needs to pay particular attention to food because the energy demands from exertion and heat production are enormous and constant.

As already mentioned, eating snack foods is one way of dealing with energy loss. That part of the menu provides regular, convenient refueling. There are many choices, but food that is hard to chew or break when frozen should be avoided. Things like small candies, beef jerky, nuts, and dried fruits are logical choices. Some of this may sound like the dream menu of a junk food addict, but in winter such things have an appropriate place. The dietary concerns we face in our sedentary lives are not a reasonable carry-over for winter. In particular, sugar has a beneficial role to play. The Indian people in the north knew this; for centuries maple sugar was part of their diet.

Snack food during the day is only part of the picture. A substantial and nourishing breakfast and dinner play an equally important role. Those meals provide slower-burning fuels that will sustain you.

Food preparation is not easy in winter. Big meals should be kept as simple as possible. I'm partial to one-pot meals—things like stew, chili, or goulash in the evening, and fortified oatmeal, hot cereal, or scrambled eggs with bacon bits for breakfast. Those one-pot meals should provide plenty of food. Don't skimp. If you use prepared trail foods, use at least a four-person pack for two people. Staying warm depends on burning food, and it is hard to maintain body heat on reduced rations.

You can easily prepare your own trail foods from dry ingredients at home. It's best if your recipe will cook up in about twenty minutes. You may have to experiment with products at home to come up with a selection of meals. Starches, carbohydrates, and fats all have a role to play and should be included. By designing your own meals you can cater to your tastes as well as boost the number of calories a meal will produce. Your big meals will have to carry a person for many hours of activity, so make them high in calories.

Diet-conscious people will find such menus frightening. Remember, though, that an active outdoor life in winter will burn calories at a prodigious rate. The body will be hungry for fuel and will burn every bit you give it.

A hot meal at the end of the day is also good for morale and makes the night feel less cold. Sharing a hot meal can be an important part of a successful winter experience because it brings people together. The stress of strenuous winter activity can cause some depression. A warm meal and quiet conversation will help rebuild both body and soul.

In fact, in times of crisis or emergency it is constructive to get food into people. Carry packets of instant soup for use in an emergency. Cooking will focus attention away from the problem, and it will resupply the body with energy. A close call affects the entire person, and it is certainly better to do something constructive, like making soup, than to sit brooding over a problem.

It is best to have more than enough food on hand for emergency situations. If you run short of food you are in real trouble. I always carry enough to last three days beyond my planned length of stay. Only rarely will a winter storm last longer than three days, and the extra food will allow you to ride the storm through.

Although I've already talked about liquids, the subject of dehydration bears mentioning again. The symptoms of dehydration are headache, fatigue, irritability, stiffness, change in skin color. If you recognize the start of symptoms you can treat the condition with liquids. Salt deprivation may occur along with dehydration, so I go a little heavier on salt in the winter.

I counteract dehydration, in part, by keeping my one-pot meals soupy, thus providing additional water for each camper. That habit has led to a pleasant discovery. At home, I precook my ingredients then drain them. Those ingredients are then sealed in a plastic bag and frozen. They will, of course, stay frozen once the trip starts, and when a meal is needed I simply empty the contents into boiling water. Cooking, then, is mainly boiling water, and I get fast, convenient meals with ample liquid content.

People often ask if it isn't possible to freeze homemade stew and cook a chunk of that. It is possible, but it is slow and the food burns easily. The method just described is easier, though it involves more effort at home.

The following menu suggestions provide some food for thought. Hopefully, they will stimulate you to invent your own special meals. The menus I suggest, however, require little cooking and are adapted to winter conditions.

Breakfast

Scrambled Eggs & Bacon. Use a dehydrated egg mix and water in a frying pan. As the eggs begin to cook, add precooked bacon (three or four strips per person, cut into pieces). A hearty portion consists of three eggs per person. Melted cheese, margarine, and other ingredients can be added to boost calories.

Hot Cereal. Oatmeal or hot cereal can be boosted by adding brown sugar, dry milk or coffee creamer, chopped nuts, or dried fruit. These mixtures will cook in a few minutes, so they are easy to prepare. The result should be a loose porridge.

Drinks. To cocoa mix add coffee creamer, tiny marshmallows, dry milk, or protein powder to fortify the cocoa. To hot, spiced tea add sugar or honey. Hot Jell-O is a drink favored by many because it contains some nutrients.

Lunch

Frozen Sandwiches. Thin, small sandwiches are more convenient than thick ones. Meaty sandwich spreads work well, too. Avoid foods that would be difficult to chew or bite off.

Other. Precut cheese or sausage pieces are both rich in fats and provide many calories. A light coating of margarine will prevent pieces from freezing together. Crackers or trail mix goes well with a cheese and sausage lunch.

Dinner

Stew. To boiling water, add precooked meat and vegetables. Small pieces will heat quicker. Add dry soup or gravy mix for more flavor. Instant rice adds bulk and texture. The meat used should be cooked in seasoning to prevent it from being bland.

Stroganoff. To boiling water add your precooked meat mixture, quick-cooking noodles, stroganoff mix, and dry milk. Sour cream mix will add flavor, if desired. The result is more like a casserole than stroganoff.

There are many other possibilities, but try to keep winter cooking as simple as possible. When I plan a winter menu I ask one question: "Can it be cooked by adding boiling water?" Strive for simple, substantial meals.

Remember, the body's demand for food will be high. Morning meals should stress protein for the day's work. Evening meals should stress carbohydrates and starches to carry you through the night.

Hazards

Fatigue and Hypothermia. I have mentioned the physical stress and exertion of winter camping. I'd like to make that more graphic. Imagine this situation: One foot of new snow covers the trail. You are traveling on snowshoes. Your stride is eighteen inches, and with each step you sink down one foot. In a mile and a half of travel you will take 5,200 one-foot vertical steps. That's nearly a mile, straight up.

In addition to that kind of exertion, there is the body's demand for heat. The combination produces strain, which can lead to fatigue.

Fatigue is dangerous. Any parent can describe what happens to a child's behavior when the child is tired and hungry. Performance, mood, decision-making are all affected. When it comes to fatigue, we are all vulnerable, regardless of age. Fatigue can be handled through rest stops, snacks, fluids, and paced exertion. However, people suffering from fatigue may not see that it's time to rest, stop, eat, or pull together. Indeed, once they feel tired, they are afraid to stop. That's where the danger comes in. Fatigue can lead to a near-panic desire to keep going.

The effects of fatigue become much worse if hypothermia is starting to affect a group. Most outdoor people have heard about hypothermia. It is a condition that involves loss of body heat. As the body cools, it adjusts by reducing the flow of blood to the extremities. It does that to conserve heat for the vital organs, located in the trunk. Unfortunately, one of the extremities that suffers is the brain. With a reduced blood flow, there is a reduction in reasoning and decision making ability.

Therein lies the *problem* of hypothermia. A person suffering from hypothermia will often insist that he is "fine." Reduced mental functioning does not allow him to see the condition. But shivers, loss of coordination, slurred speech, and slow response are serious signs. If even one person in a group has those signs, it is time for the group to stop, eat, build a fire, and (very likely) make camp for the day.

Making camp early may not be in the plan, but it is the correct thing to do. First, if one person is showing signs of hypothermia, it is likely that one or two others are approaching it, too. Second, the condition does not go away without treatment; continuing to travel makes things worse. The person must be warmed up and given food and drink promptly. Eskimo and Indian people would undress and use direct body heat to warm a chilled person. In the bush, this is often the fastest method of warming.

It should be emphasized that alcohol makes the start of hypothermia quicker. Alcohol speeds up heat loss in the extremities and it further dulls the reasoning portion of the brain. These things only aggravate the symptoms of hypothermia. Alcohol does not warm a person up. The camper who insists on "just a little drink" is making a big mistake. For my part, alcohol has no place on any winter trip.

I want to make it clear that fatigue and hypothermia can have a combined effect. Dehydration (which has already been mentioned) and the use of alcohol are part of the same set of symptoms and problems. Any one of these factors can cause serious trouble by itself. But in the early stages they can combine for a quick, dramatic loss of function. It can sneak up on an individual or a group, and things can fall apart quickly. A moderate pace and *early* prevention are the most reliable defense.

I've said things can fall apart. Let me give an example. People who are part of rescue squads often describe the search for a lost hunter as a chase. They say it isn't so much a matter of finding the person as it is of catching him. Cold and fatigue combine to foster blind, irrational fear. One symptom of hypothermia is panic. The evidence shows that even people who are experienced and prepared simply fail to take the right steps once they are stricken with hypothermia. Panicked and unable to regain control of themselves, they run until they drop.

I want to make it clear that knowing the symptoms is in no way a defense against them or their effects. Knowledge about hypothermia does not prevent a reduced flow of blood to the brain if you become badly chilled. The real danger of hypothermia and its relatives is that knowledge will not be brought into play once the symptoms begin to show. The expert winter camper is as vulnerable as the novice. That is why a moderate pace and prevention are so important. The problem is loss of physical and mental function—once that starts, it tends to take over.

Each winter camper must be cautioned to obey any decision to stop travel and regroup. Obedience is important, and with it goes the realization that we can spot a decline of performance in others, but not in ourselves. Remember, the nature of the problem is such that we will not relaize it is happening to us.

Sometimes people in a group want to say, "Let those three go on ahead. The rest of us will catch up later." That's dangerous. It's a poor idea to divide the team. When people and supplies are separated, the potential for trouble is greater. The winter camper must recognize the value of obedience, and he must also see the value of staying and working together.

If you combine the evidence, you can see how it adds up. Someone in the group had a cold the week before and they are not fully over it. There has been an energy-robbing wind all day. Add a restless night, damp feet, soaked mittens, and you have the makings of more serious trouble. Such little things add up, and they drain people's energy and their ability to perform.

You can be sure, too, that many people will suffer in silence. They don't want to be a *bother* or a problem for others in the group. Well, I'd rather be bothered by a living person who can recover, than have the bother of having to haul out a body. It is not a bother to take action to conserve life and energy.

It is surprising to see how seldom people are willing to admit to discomfort or weakness. Yet, accepting those feelings, reporting them, and acting on them is important. When people agree to obedience during a winter trip, they must also agree to give an accurate report of their own condition.

It's not unusual for people to expect more from a wilderness trip, more from their bodies, and more from their minds than is realistic. One step toward a safe trip is mental preparation. In part, this involves the recognition of physical feelings—of human limits. Feeling a little tired means it's time for a break. Feeling thirsty means it's time for water. Feeling sore leg muscles means it's time to ease off and not aggravate that condition. You can't expect a decent trip if the body is abused or ignored. Listen to your body. Mentally prepare yourself to heed what your body says. A body and mind in harmony may be the best reward of your trip.

Staying Dry. Loss of function is greatly increased if you get wet. The moderate pace I've recommended helps to prevent getting wet from overheating and sweating. Once you get too wet, the wind chill will cut right through you. Rest breaks, which allow the body to ventilate and cool, are crucial. Strenuous stretches should be done slowly, without getting too wet.

Be constantly alert to the possiblity of getting damp. Don't sit in the snow. Avoid falls, and stay away from open water. Steer away from slushy areas. Frequently brush or shake snow from your clothing before the sun, radiant heat from the fire, or your body's own radiation cause it to dampen your clothes. Staying dry is far better than trying to dry out.

Staying dry is much more difficult during a warm spell. Warm snaps make overheating easier, and the snow you come into contact with is closer to melting temperature. The best temperature for winter camping is about zero degrees Fahrenheit. At that temperature a person can work hard without overheating as easily, and snow will not melt on contact with clothing.

Another natural condition that can make you wet is a snowstorm. Snowfalls usually occur during warm conditions involving warm, moist air meeting a cold high. With temperatures at or near freezing, the falling snow often will melt as soon as it hits your body. A person can become soaked and find himself in serious trouble in an hour. Travel in a snowstorm is best avoided. Some storms create poor visibility as well, and your best chance is to make camp and stay put.

It is also best to make camp if you become lost. Searchers will find it harder to locate you if you keep moving. Give them a chance to find you.

In the meantime your job is to wait, conserve energy, and utilize the resources at your disposal.

In that regard, too, it is never wise to separate yourself from your equipment. If you fear being snowed in, it is tempting to take off and leave the equipment so you can travel faster and easier. Doing so, however, has only one satisfactory outcome—either you get all the way to safety or you lose. It's not rare, you know, for people to freeze to death short distances from a haven they hadn't the strength to reach. Certainly, when you first start off you'll be warm and dry. But you have to look ahead and think about what your condition is likely to be when you're halfway there. Also, you know you *can* survive with your equipment—and you know you *cannot* survive without it. The safe decision is obvious.

Style

At first glance, the topic of style appears to have little to do with winter camping. However, questions of style do relate. First, there is style in clothing. The clothing I have described isn't very stylish. People currently turning toward outdoor winter activity are being exposed to clothing that is both colorful and stylish. It is logical for them to ask, "Why can't I buy my winter camping clothes at a ski shop? Do I have to look like a logger, too?" The two styles, that of the ski shop and that of the logger, have two different functions.

Ski clothing for cross-country (such as knickers and body suits) is designed to dump excess heat from the body. It is relatively tight fitting, and it allows for more rapid radiation of excess heat and moisture. Ski clothing is well suited for fast-paced free skiing. The clothing I recommend is suitable for a slower pace and longer term exposure to the elements.

Ski clothing is warm as long as the wearer maintains a fairly high level of activity. That's fine for short-term jaunts, where you will return home and be able to change. It is not appropriate for winter camping. It is unwise to base staying warm on continual high exertion. That's a difficult program to maintain day after day on a winter camping trip. And such a program assumes that nothing will go wrong. The margin of safety is too thin when anything less than all-out skiing will leave the person feeling cold.

I've had people say to me, "Well, I'll ski hard during the day and put on warmer clothes when we make camp." That assumes, of course, that warm clothes are not needed during the day. It assumes, too, that changing in the bush is as easy as changing clothes at home. Do you change clothes before you make camp or after the tents are up and your gear's unpacked? Assumptions don't address questions of a practical nature, and they conveniently ignore the rigors of winter. You'd be surprised how tired and irrational people can become after a day of braving the elements. They drag into camp with little energy for anything. So, a style of clothing that adds to physical strain is risky. You can't assume that after taking such a risk you will be in good enough shape to camp safely.

My recommendation is that you dress warmer to begin with and reduce your level of exertion accordingly. This leaves you with enough reserve energy to complete the day's activity and make adequate preparations for night. Be warned that simply taking it easy on a cold day with a light breeze requires a great deal of energy. We all have physical limits, and a good plan will keep us from reaching those limits.

Another question of style concerns your approach to both skiing and winter camping. A slow, conservative, thoughtful approach that respects winter is best. A travel or camping style that stresses raw endurance (roughing it), mileage, and achievement probably involves taking risks. The north woods won't even notice if you live or die out there. Needless risks hurt you and your trip, and they prove nothing. Getting psyched-up to contend against the elements simply pushes the issue onto dangerous ground. The enemy is not the stabbing cold so much as it is our reluctance to accept it and take appropriate measures.

The question of style is important because some styles are more appropriate for wilderness than others. Most of us learn the basics under relatively safe conditions, and our style reflects that. People come north for a few days of recreation, and they bring a style of activity with them. Most often, their style is fast and hard—they want to make the most of every moment and do as much as possible. That style, particularly for cross-country skiers, can mean trouble.

The style you use should be suitable for the location as well as for the activity. I've seen people come off a five-mile ski loop soaking wet from perspiration. I've seen them take off at night for a jaunt on skis before bed— hard, sweaty skiing, with temperatures sinking, no help around, and darkness to confound them or anyone searching for them. You have to remember *where* you are. You are not on the local golf course; help may be hours away. Remember, too, that racing-style skiing is suitable under controlled conditions, on a prepared track where dangers are fewer. That will not be the case up north. If you lose your way, break a ski tip, or underestimate your travel time, the racing style can leave you wringing wet and in trouble.

I am compelled to be forceful and blunt about safety for winter outings. The environment *is* harsh. Losing fingers or toes to frostbite *is* tragic. Being too casual about the risks of wilderness travel in winter *is* a mistake. Not that we would make the mistake on purpose. But mistakes happen when we are over-eager or naive about what conditions are like or what our equipment can do. Any one of us can miss something obvious, so it is important that we slow ourselves down and catch our faulty thinking before it leads to tragedy.

Take your time and work through all the stages and steps required for winter camping. Doing so is part of a learning process. If you succumb to the urge to rush out and buy everything you'll need, you are probably short-cutting the process and going too quickly. Your entire style must become adjusted to winter. Style of travel, camping, thinking, and planning all has to be reviewed. A good review will take time, and it will become more valid as you gain knowledge and experience. In time, your appreciation of winter will include a balanced awareness of the ways in which it can promote respect and fear as well as relaxation and enjoyment. When you feel that balance, the appropriate style for winter has become part of you.

Family Winter Camping

Winter camping sounds like something for athletes, but with moderation in mind, it may be well suited to the average family. Certainly, physical ability and a degree of fitness is required. If you exercise and lead an active life, then you can reasonably work toward attempting a winter camping trip. If you are inactive and out of shape, then your first step is to work on fitness. Likewise, very young children are not ready for this sort of thing. However, winter camping is not something just for a special few. (Indeed, if your camping plan could only be carried out by conditioned, serious athletes on a mission, then your plan may well be unreasonably demanding. If your plan could be considered unsafe for a healthy preteen it's probably not safe for an adult tired from a long day's skiing.)

Getting ready for winter camping begins with doing little things together. There are short jaunts to take for day trips, which can be enjoyed by young and old, family and friends. If your emphasis is on experiencing and learning (rather than on high performance), you'll have a versatile approach suitable for a wide range of people. The basics can be practiced or tried out under any convenient situation that allows people to experiment a little at a time, without being committed to spending a week in the wilderness.

That's reasonable. After all, not everyone in your family will be interested. This way they have a chance to discover what is right for them. Winter camping should not be forced on anyone. But the process of working toward a winter camping trip can form a portion of your family recreational plan.

The next step may be a stay at a resort in the area where you would some-day like to camp. Again, do things that can be done during the day and re-turn to the resort for the night. Improve your skills while expanding your base of familiarity and experience. Don't push the issue of camping out. When people start to feel ready they will move in that direction without being pushed. In the meantime, you can't blame them for being cautious about something like winter camping. The cautious ones are the ones you can trust on a trip.

After a few winters of gaining experience and building skills, you are ready for something more ambitious. Your foundation is ready, but taking the step is bound to provoke doubts and questions. Have we got the right gear? Are the kids too young? What did we forget? If you didn't have those questions you wouldn't be headed toward safe winter camping. Your doubts are a good sign—evidence of practical concern.

Whether you are ready or not is something you have to decide for your-self. If you've a good foundation, the pieces will work into place. If your doubts remain serious and lasting, then it is likely that more foundation work is in order.

One limitation on family trips is the ratio of adults to children. By the time kids get to be teens, they can make a reasonable contribution. It's best to have two capable adults for every younger person. You must, however, avoid a situation where the workload falls too heavily on a few people. If you lack sufficient adult power, try checking with a church group, scout troop, outing club, or some other organization to locate interested people.

With a balanced group, you are ready. The first winter campout should be conducted close to a safe base, such as a cabin or resort. Don't travel far from your base. Concentrate on making camp, preparing for the night, and taking short side trips. Part of your group may elect to return indoors for the night. That's fine. If even a few stay outdoors overnight, the whole group gains from the experience. You'll go through a lot of work for such a small step, but it's a step in the right direction.

There is plenty to learn from small steps. At the very least, your summer camping ability will be improved by facing the rigors of winter. Such exper-ience is useful at all ages. The safety consciousness and body awareness that results helps build fine outdoor users.

The concept of family winter camping may strike you as being overly op-timistic. But if your plan isn't safe for the kids, then your plan is not safe, *period*. If it is suitable for a range of ages, then you probably have a work-able design. The harshness of winter makes it clear that sleep, food, and cooperation are basic at all ages. A degree from the university of winter of-fers a vivid message. In the most rigorous season, the beauty of simple, outdoor living is a profound experience. Along those lines there is something else I want to mention. An interest in the outdoors is something that never leaves a person. Not everyone has a strong attraction for wild country, but for those who do, its meaning will endure for a lifetime. I can't explain my own attraction for wild places. No words have ever been sufficient for the feeling, but I know others share it.

You can help uncover those people and in so doing make a special contribution. Winter camping can lead to new friendships or to new insights about those already in your life. The parents or relatives who get the kids out camping may not learn for years how important their efforts were. The youth who cajoles his parents into trying cross-country skiing may make an important contribution to their better health. The family that drags Uncle Charlie along on an outing may revive his long-dead interest in the outdoors. You've heard old Tom's stories about his Civilian Conservation Corps days, but have you heard him tell them sitting near the place that was so much a part of his youth?

You can be sure there is some purpose behind your interest in winter camping. The worthwhile results can reach over years and lifetimes. If you look back at your own history it is often possible to spot some occurrence that started you down a long, productive path. In life or in camping, it works the same way. The opportunity is there. The frozen trees and ice-bound lakes don't benefit from our camping, so the benefit must lie with us. It's a new kind of adventure to sow seeds of opportunity in the garden of winter. It is an intimately human adventure, and one that is right and needful at any age.

Applications

It's not necessary to be an expert winter camper to learn something from winter. The lessons are not aimed at a special segment of society. They apply to the basics of life for all of us. So, I feel confident that what winter camping has to teach us has a wider application.

Knowledge of winter camping will rub off on camping situations in other seasons. Even a little winter experience will sharpen camping skills in general. Attention to detail and a keen awareness of obvious health and safety matters are also benefits. In particular, it's important to remember the dangers of fatigue, hypothermia, and dehydration. We are most aware of them in winter, but they occur in *all* seasons. In fact, most exposure (hypothermia) cases occur in spring and fall, but they can happen nearly as easily on a wet, windy day in summer.

The physical nature of our bodies is constant. We know that physical stress can affect moods and reasoning, so, dealing with it is a matter of considerable practical concern. This is true in all seasons, all climates, all zones, at all times. Exhaustion caused by exertion in the bush requires attention just as does fatigue brought on by pressure at work. Both affect us in a very real way.

Aside from improved camping skills and a sharpened awareness of health and safety matters, familiarity with winter camping and survival brings new perspective. You can't, for example, help but gain respect for prehistoric peoples who lived face to face with the elements year-round. Our ventures into outdoor winter living are made only after detailed planning and careful assessment. Prehistoric people camped out routinely. Can we still call their ability to live out of doors "primitive"?

Living well under difficult circumstances stimulates a wide range of our interests and abilities. It is certainly more stimulating and dynamic than going to the average movie or bowling a few rounds. The experience is so direct and powerful that it prompts insight in unexpected ways. After all, it places the emphasis on our human resources, and that's not typical in our consumer society. Productive winter camping can't be bought; it can only be lived or experienced. Nature's season of cold and dormancy is the exact opposite for us—as we experience it, we become productive and we grow. We are forced to reach inside ourselves, uncovering the best that's in us. In winter's great white wilderness there is room for as much humanity as we are capable of.

That brings me to the social side of winter camping. Hard times bring about a spontaneous recognition of what society and community are all about. A few winter days spent in the bush with people offers a mini-lesson in practical, human government. Such a society may be small, closed, or even artificial, but it is still instructive. The cooperative efforts required in order to cope with winter's demands make it apparent that each of us has something to give and something to receive.

Fortunately, it's not necessary to be an academic or an expert to function well or to heed winter's lessons. The experience is open to all. Sharing time, energy, enthusiasm, and hope gives us a chance to discover what we each have to offer.

Winter is a harsh master. It pushes us. It even causes us grief. But it has its rewards. The cold wind doesn't douse the fire inside. It's like discovering love—love so deep and true it will accept "sorrow" as well as "joy." Such love says, "Even though I don't get just what I want and every detail doesn't please me, I still love having every minute of this opportunity."

It's ironic that winter can bring so much out of people. Does the cold outdoors force us to find more warmth and humanity within? Whatever the cause, the rosy-cheeked smiles of winter are genuine.

Your trip into winter will, hopefully, lead you to your own form of genuine discovery. The actual trip may start on skis or snowshoes, but somewhere along the way you will discover wings. That's the bounty of winter. It helps the spirit to journey on. That journey, part vision-dream-reality, is something the soul yearns for. You'll feel your spirit joyously take wing—when they ask you why your eyes are wet, tell them it must be the wind.

Equipment Checklist

The checklist is fairly complete. Obviously, not everything is used on every trip; the list has a range of applications. I encourage the use of a checklist. Check and recheck each item. Be methodical and take your time; that's good insurance toward a safer trip. A tear-out equipment list is printed on page 103.

Checklist

ITEM	Checked	Rechecked
Clothing		
Long underwear & spares	_____	_____
Wool pants, suspenders, belt	_____	_____
Shirt	_____	_____
Handkerchief & spare	_____	_____
Snowmobile boots & spare liners	_____	_____
Ski boots, gaiters, overboots	_____	_____
Vest	_____	_____
Wool Jacket	_____	_____
Down Jacket & hood	_____	_____
Goggles or sunglasses	_____	_____
Chapstick	_____	_____
Wool socks & spares	_____	_____
Mitts, liners, & spares	_____	_____
Hat, wool cap, face mask	_____	_____
Quilted underwear set	_____	_____
Other_____	_____	_____
Other_____	_____	_____
Travel Equipment		
Skis & poles	_____	_____
Snowshoes	_____	_____
Wax kit, ski tip, etc.	_____	_____

ITEM	Checked	Rechecked
Towing toboggan & poles	_____	_____
Push-bar	_____	_____
Foam blocks	_____	_____
Pack frame	_____	_____
Spare parts & tool bag	_____	_____
Other_____	_____	_____
Other_____	_____	_____

Camping Equipment

	Checked	Rechecked
4-person Eureka Timberlines	_____	_____
Timberline vestibules	_____	_____
Versa Tarp groundcloth	_____	_____
Steel spikes	_____	_____
Wind tarp or Versa Tarp	_____	_____
Cord	_____	_____
Candle lanterns & candles	_____	_____
Camp shovels	_____	_____
Axe & saw	_____	_____
Cooking grate	_____	_____
Fire Starter	_____	_____
Duluth No. 3 Cruiser packs	_____	_____
Coleman Peak stove, fuel, filter	_____	_____
Cook kit, silverware, etc.	_____	_____
Dishpan	_____	_____
Thermos & liner	_____	_____
Food pack *plus three days food*	_____	_____
Map, compass, etc.	_____	_____
Recreation (camera, fishing, etc.)	_____	_____

ITEM	Checked	Rechecked
Liquid soap, matches, etc.	_____	_____
Other_____	_____	_____
Other_____	_____	_____

Sleeping Equipment

	Checked	Rechecked
Duluth No. 3 Cruiser packs	_____	_____
(approx. 1 per person)		
Sleeping bag/bags	_____	_____
Thermal liners	_____	_____
Foam pads (3 per 2 people)	_____	_____
Wool blanket or flannel cover	_____	_____
Other_____	_____	_____
Other_____	_____	_____

Automobile

	Checked	Rechecked
Jumper cables	_____	_____
Tire chains	_____	_____
Cold starting carb spray	_____	_____
Window scraper	_____	_____
Large shovel	_____	_____
Carriers	_____	_____
Other_____	_____	_____
Other_____	_____	_____

Around the Protective Fire

Around the Protective Fire

Minnesotans joke about winter. One lifelong resident used to say, "We've only got two seasons here, winter and the Fourth of July." A Swede who came here as a young man was fond of saying, "We got nine months of winter, and three months of poor sledding."

Silly jokes, I know, but on long winter nights people think up such things. They are part of our local tradition because they allow us to chuckle at winter, which so often frustrates our plans or forces us to take extraordinary measures.

Quite obviously, those same winter nights provide an opportunity for people to get together. When we're not out ice-fishing or testing our four-wheelers against the elements, swapping stories and anecdotes with friends is a popular pastime. Tales shared round the fire are an essential part of camping out in the bush, as if the intensity of the cold led to a more intense personal experience which could be shared with others.

Around the protective fire or in the snug home of a friend, we swap stories and information. Our exchanges, too, sometimes lean toward reflection, for winter gives us a chance to catch our breath after the busy season of summer. Time given to reflection is time for taking stock. In some cases, our stock will be a silly joke; in other cases, a detailed plan thoroughly researched over an entire winter, or a sudden realization about an event that happened months before when we were too busy to grasp its full importance.

Even a devoted winter camper cannot spend every moment outdoors. There is a need for time spent at the hearth, at a stable base of operations, a haven. Coming home brings a heartfelt appreciation for convenience after the more rigorous life of the bush. At least it works that way for this winter camper, who finds further meaning in winter camping when reflecting on it from the safety of a snug indoor setting.

The pieces that follow are not exclusively about winter camping. Rather, they are reflections and observations about winter or triggered by winter moods—a sampling of the sorts of items talked about round the fire. I welcome you into that ring of light with me.

Other Seasons

Fall and spring are what we normally call the seasons surrounding winter, but do you know those seasons by their northern names? From my home in the north, I've come to adopt the same sorts of names for the seasons that the Ojibway people used. They had a season called Berry (blueberry) and Mano-Min (wild rice) Months. Another was called Broken Snowshoe and Boiling (of maple sap) Months. The descriptive, northern way of saying fall is Wild Rice Season, for spring it's Maple Syrup Season.

I'll start with Wild Rice Season, which is the prelude to winter. The snow season doesn't come all at once; it arrives in stages.

The first stage comes as the rice begins to ripen. Days are still warm and sunny. Nights will start to become frosty before there's any sign of hard-freezing. A few trees will be "early"—they turn color well before the rest, as if they can't wait to proclaim the season with a burst of wind-rustled flamboyance. Water reeds start to turn brown, and water levels are often the lowest they will be all year. You can't see winter approach, but you know it's nearer as fall develops, much as the rice does.

Imperceptibly at first, the rice fills out. The green heads of rice take on a slightly swollen appearance, though they are still mostly air. A few days pass and the husks fill with a milky, saplike paste. If all goes well, the paste will solidify and darken into ripe rice. Almost overnight the rice becomes ready for harvest, and sometimes there is only a day or two when harvesting is possible.

The season for harvesting is short and unpredictable. Each year brings a new twist to a familiar overall pattern. Some years the rice will surprise you and be excellent when you don't expect it to be. Sometimes the husks will be mostly empty, even though they are plentiful. Other years, rice worms are more abundant than the rice. Ducks on the move may drop in and eat a field bare in an evening. A pre-winter storm may blow in, high winds and sleety rain knocking the rice into the water before it can be harvested. Ricing time is always the same—unpredictable and educational.

When a person lives close to the land, he begins to pay attention to these natural lessons. They form part of a larger pattern that grows in meaning as the years accumulate. I've logged days in the rice marshes that were hardly worth the effort. And I've seen days when the rice falls into the canoe like drifting snow and one day's harvest is more than you'd get in two or three normal seasons. You just have to accept what happens. The yearly experience is part of the total lesson.

How you rice is part of the lesson, too. Harvesting rice is hand work—the system has remained unchanged for centuries, because there's not much *to* change. Hand harvesting from a canoe being slowly poled through the marsh is just sloppy enough to insure that some rice will be lost for seed and some will be left for wildlife. Wild rice is managed wilderness-style, which means that only simple methods of harvest are allowed. The growth and harvest of wild rice follows ancient models, making ricing more than just an occupation or a means of gathering food; it's a way of looking at life.

To learn more about rice and its role, I've talked to people. I tracked down one old man in Canada. People said he knew a lot about the bush, but that he was dangerous, maybe a little crazy. I found his place, introduced myself, told him I wanted to talk about wild rice. His eyes lit up and he said, "Mano-Min, huh? It's more than food, you know. Kept me and my family alive for years. Come on in."

The old-timer led me into his clean, compact shack where he had a coffee pot sitting on an airtight stove. He told me about Mano-Min (wild rice), his wife, his daughters and son. Information poured from him, a simple, dignified man who met most of his own needs and who piled wood neater than anyone I've ever encountered. He had much to give, and I provide here a glimmer of what he had to offer.

He told me that when they had a good year, his Ojibway wife and he would try to get enough rice to last five seasons. He said he had learned this from his wife's people, who had taught him that you couldn't count on getting good rice every year, but if you planned ahead you could count on it somewhere along the line.

A bad year for rice might be a good year for fall fishing. He said the people looked for that sort of balance when they lived with the land. But you had to live close to the land and respect its decisions. The old-timer then looked thoughtful. He said something in Ojibway that apparently didn't translate well into English. He was struggling to put Indian wisdom into a form I could understand. Giving me a serious look, he said, "The old people knew so much. When things were going bad, you'd go to them. In a while, one of them would remember something and they'd tell you what to try. The old people had listened to the land for many years. They knew what it said."

That's important. To make peace with the land, we must listen to it. Part of listening involves hearing the wisdom of those who have listened longer.

It's not easy to do, though. Listening to wisdom is often difficult for us. Learning to accept the "rightness" of lean years isn't an overnight lesson. Where do we get the resiliency to bounce back and say, "Well, there was no wild rice this year, but it's a good fall for cutting firewood"? Maybe, in a small way, we gain simply by using new labels for "old" seasons, transforming ordinary old fall into Wild Rice Season, or Firewood Time, or Hawk Watching Months, or Color Appreciation Days. A new label might help us see a new opportunity.

Spring, already a time for transformation, undergoes further transformation when it's called Maple Syrup Season. All winter the maples hold their sugar in readiness for spring. The land is dormant, and the woods are deep in snow. It's still cold at night, and a reasonable person could hardly claim that spring had started. But the maples know more about spring than I do, and when it looks for all the world like winter, they announce spring by releasing their sweet sap.

Cold nights, and days above freezing, bring a good flow of sap. But the season isn't predictable. A sudden spring will have a short flow and lead to early budding on the trees. A delayed spring may start normally and then turn cold, leaving all your equipment hanging frozen and useless on the trees. And, of course, there are lots of seasons that fall between good and bad.

The work involved is considerable. The sap has to be hauled from tree to tree as you collect it. Sometimes the trails are firm, but a warm day will turn the packed snow into liquid mush. When the trails break up, the work is grueling and frustrating, especially when a treacherous section of trail trips you and you dump ten gallons of sap—all your effort trickling away. Of course, something like that happens when you're nearly to the truck where you'd have poured the sap into a holding tank.

After the sap is collected, the next step is to boil it down. The Ojibway people knew exactly how to describe spring by calling it Broken Snowshoe and Boiling Months, because there's lots of boiling to do. It takes roughly 40 gallons of sap to make 1 gallon of syrup. Most of what you haul out of the woods goes up in steam. I don't produce syrup on a large scale, mind you, but on one of the poorer seasons I had only 2½ gallons of syrup for a week's efforts. You'd better believe that I placed considerable value on that syrup. It almost seemed a shame to pour it on pancakes.

I'm glad to have put in a few seasons doing maple syrup. It's given me new slants on spring, on what nature has to provide, on what needs to be done to harvest nature in a responsible way. I've learned about economy of effort and splendid waste—all at the same time. It's brought me closer to the past and to the way of life followed by Indian people who tapped trees as a part of their lifestyle rather than as a hobby. It's given me more appreciation for the north country—its sweetness and the effort needed to enjoy it.

The work and ideas associated with wild rice and maple syrup seasons remind me of an inclusive, broad management plan for wild lands, a plan that does not rely on single seasons or an exclusive style of management for individual crops. I think of this as wilderness-style management. Wilderness-style management requires that we not utilize one resource at the expense of other resources.

The difficulty in adopting wilderness-style management arises from the fact that it focuses on multiple resources, a more complex task than focussing on single resource management. It would, for example, be fairly easy to manage wild land for timber alone, planting trees in rows at an optimal distance to foster fast growth. Such a single resource plan would become yet more efficient if all competing growth that might rob nutrients from the trees were eliminated. And of course, any wildlife that was harmful to trees would have to be exterminated, as would all destructive insects. But management for a single resource has serious drawbacks and awesome repercussions for the environment. I would avoid these problems by not treating nature as a single thing or single product.

The wilderness style and the desire to note "other seasons," that is, to be aware of the many different things our natural resources have to offer, yields a sympathetic approach to management. With it, we come on foot, willing to cooperate, seeking to act in concert with nature's broader workings. We seek to harvest, but when what can be harvested physically is limited, a wilderness style encourages us to shift our goals. As much of our harvest comes from within as from without when we work with nature in a way that allows us to listen to the land.

If these words sound idealistic, I can tell you that I have as much trouble putting them into action as does anyone else. I run a business guiding canoe trips. After one or two good seasons, I expect the third one to be even better, and when it turns out to be slow, I have to scratch around like anyone else. New opportunities often look like problems and troubles when they first show themselves. In the case of my business, the problem of a slow year for canoe trips was turned into more time for staff training and greater emphasis on archaeological research, both long-term investments. Instead of ruining my business, the problems encountered have forced me to add new things to it.

As a guide, I work with people, and I hear their stories. Sometimes they mention a difficulty, or even a tragedy, that caused a central, inner change in how and why they lived. What happened for them isn't a lot different from what I have had to learn through my business. I've come to know that difficulty can be turned into opportunity. Something inside a person opens when a fresh face is put on an old problem. Problems, then, become other seasons—new seasons.

It's hard to think of fall as a time of decline when you see wild rice ripen and reach fulfillment. Winter isn't dead-time when you know it's a time for pulling around the fire with those important in your life. Each season has many facets. Winter may seem lifeless, but it's really a preparation for renewed life. What happens in the physical world is mirrored in the inner world of each person. The reflective, quiet times of winter prepare us and give us the desire for spring and all its demands. Like nature, we bounce back with life and energy. We may not change the world from snow white to green, as nature does, but we can feel a comparable change inside ourselves. After all, only a portion of the season exists outside—the other part, the other season, dwells within.

"What Was That?"

It was a late afternoon in October when it happened. There was no warning. I came around a curve on the bumpy sawmill road, and there it was. My neighbor, Jeff, was riding in the pickup with me, and he saw it, too. As I recall, we both reacted at nearly the same moment.

He said, "A deer."

I said, "Moose."

Even as I said "moose," though, I was changing my mind, because I'd never seen a moose show a white flag (like a whitetailed deer) at its rear. Jeff was having a similar problem with his interpretation, and he said something to the effect that he'd "never seen a deer with a rack like that."

I was trying to drive and look at the same time. The animal moved off the road and stepped into a patch of hazel brush, so although we got closer our view was obscured. All the while, my head kept going from "moose" to "deer," but neither label seemed right. It was as if whatever it was had to be some sort of cross between a deer and a moose. But there wasn't anything like that, was there? As the creature disappeared into the trees I still had no clear idea of what I'd seen.

Neither did Jeff. We both said, "What *was* that?" at the same time.

Jeff told me it had reminded him of the elk he'd seen out West. When he said elk, I thought of caribou. Elk are not native to the region, but caribou had been at one time. However, there had been no caribou in Minnesota for a long time—nearly fifty years. It wasn't likely to be either an elk or a caribou, so what was it? When I got home I wrote down what Jeff and I had agreed on as a description:

1. The color was too dark for a deer.
2. The size was bulky, but not more than three times the size of a deer.
3. It had a rack with both palms and spikes—as if the rack was part moose and part deer.
4. It had a bold, white patch on the rear.
5. The chest color was light.
6. The fur above the hooves was light.

Only one animal looks like that. A mammal field guide confirmed that our description matched that of a caribou. Still, I didn't want to go off the deep end by claiming to have seen a caribou, which could turn out to be a neighbor's missing horse. I decided to check my facts.

The next morning I drove back to where we'd seen the animal on the dirt road. I got out and looked for tracks. Happily, I was in luck! The road had been soft that afternoon, but it had frozen solid at night. The tracks were crisp and clear. I compared the tracks in the road to those drawn in the mammal field guide. The ones on the road were caribou, all right. They'd get less clear as the day warmed and the road got muddy, but looking at them that morning I was sure they were caribou tracks.

Being sure was one thing. Being sure enough to make a report of the sighting was an entirely different matter, though. I mean, this is a rural area, and I know dozens of people who have claimed to have seen strange things in the woods. The following list will give you a sample: mountain lion, (one of the more popular things to report); Dahl sheep; California condor; whale, (in Lake Superior); and abominable snowman, (in a valley north of Hovland). You see the problem—namely, many wildlife stories are false, the sort of thing you hear from a guy who's had one-too-many. (Those same people are inclined to see UFO's, too.)

I kicked it around for a day or two before I reported my sighting. The wildlife officer I talked to was polite and considerate. He took my information, said he'd check on it and then let me know. His voice struck me as being a little too controlled, though, as if he'd heard this sort of thing *many* times before.

He called the next day. "I looked over the area," he said, "but all I found were moose tracks. I don't see much point in going any further with this, do you?"

He was right, of course. There are many moose in the area, and the "caribou" tracks I'd seen had been thawed and frozen several times when he saw them, each freeze-thaw cycle making the tracks less precise. There was just no way to confirm caribou on such flimsy evidence. I was disappointed, but there was nothing to do. The mammal field guide remained on the kitchen windowsill, a sketch drawing I'd made of the tracks sticking out from its pages.

A few weeks later, in November, a friend spent the day scouting prior to deer season. Later in the day, his scouting finished, he stopped at my place where we sat in the kitchen, drank coffee, and talked about wildlife. He noticed the field guide on the windowsill. Casually, he asked, "What are those tracks you've got drawn there?" Cautiously, I told him about my caribou sighting.

He listened, smiled, showed more and more interest. "I'll be!" he said. "I saw tracks like that today, can't be more than two miles from where you saw your caribou. There are lots of those tracks in the fresh snow. What's more, I thought they were moose tracks, but the droppings with the tracks were shaped funny and not nearly as large as moose turds."

The next day, the two of us were out looking the area over. We found tracks and droppings that matched those in Murie's excellent *Field Guide To Animal Tracks*. Even better, we found, just as Murie had described, places where the animals had pawed the ground searching for caribou moss. It looked like a sure thing, and this time there was more proof.

Again, I phoned the wildlife officer. He took my information and said he'd look into it. That night, it snowed.

Two days later the officer called back to tell me, "Sorry, all we could find up there were moose tracks and signs of moose browsing in the brush."

"Wait," I said, "I know the tracks look a lot like moose tracks, but didn't you see any of the places where the animals dug for moss?"

"No," I heard, "all we found was moose sign and bedding craters made where deer had bedded down."

If I kept pushing the issue, I'd soon be either a nuisance or a crank or both. I decided to forget the whole thing. But that's when fate stepped in and introduced me to a young man who had worked the year before on a federal wildlife project. He heard the story, went with me into the bush, saw the same sign we'd discovered earlier. That night he called his old boss and asked for advice.

Inside a few weeks, the U.S. Fish and Wildlife Service was flying over the area (after receiving financial help from the Safari Club International). The area would be surveyed from the air and they'd take pictures of wild-life.

A few days after their flight, I got a call. "We spotted caribou," I was told, "and are sending you a few pictures."

That was happy news! It felt good to know my observation had been right all along. It felt good to have been persistent (and lucky) enough to get con-firmation. Best of all, though, was knowing that caribou were back in the north country.

Other times that winter, I saw caribou in the bush. The second and third times I could appreciate what I was seeing. Caribou are snow-country ani-mals, with feet like snowshoes. The caribou's gait was proud and impres-sive. I felt fortunate to be able to observe them on part of their home range after their absence.

Unfortunately, caribou are not making a strong comeback. They are still rare in the area, their reappearance possibly a freak occurrence. The chances of caribou re-establishing themselves are tenuous at best—not so the factors that led to their demise.

During the fur trade, and later, during the logging era, moose and caribou meat was a staple. The woodland caribou came under particular pressure because caribou would form herds, making a tempting target because of the large quantities of meat that could be had at one time. The meat, I'm told, sold for 3 to 5 cents per pound. Pressure from hunting, and environmental changes caused by extensive logging, drove caribou from Minnesota.

As I researched the caribou, I came across some interesting facts. Before Europeans arrived on the scene, Indian settlements shared territory with caribou herds, and caribou flesh was frequently utilized, as was sinew, fat, and nearly all the animal. Of special importance was caribou fur, which is hollow, much like our new, synthetic fibers. Caribou robes provided excel-lent insulation for winter clothing, bedding, survival. Moose and deer hairs are solid—only the caribou provides such warmth for winter use.

The fate of caribou in the region is uncertain. Perhaps the Boundary Waters Wilderness will support a small population of our native wildlife. I hope so. I hope, too, that someday you or your children will see a caribou roaming its home range and not have such sightings be rare.

Wild Land

Earlier this winter I put on my skis, went down Pine Lake, and stopped to rest at a campsite I've used many times during summer outings. Out of curiosity, I guess, I wanted to see what the site was like covered in snow, so I climbed the bank and skied toward the tenting area. I'd only taken a few strides when a ruffed grouse exploded from its hiding place in the snow. I knew what it was, but a grouse taking off with a racket and flurry when you're not expecting it is always startling. Chuckling to myself, I looked at the place where the grouse had launched itself. This grouse had left an excellent, delicate impression of his wings, something I've always wanted to try to photograph, even though I know it's way too subtle for film.

From there I continued my slow tour of the campsite. I can't describe how odd I felt being there. My summer memories were alien to the winter setting. The convenient, flat-topped rock I'd so often used as a coffee table was drifted over with snow, only a hint of the useful rock visible. The site, empty of people and of any sign of people, looked unusually vacant, devoid of meaning. Where I'd last laid out, naked, relaxed after a swim and enjoying the warm sun on the rocks, there were deep drifts and jagged edges of shore ice that expansion pressure had forced up.

In its empty state, I felt there was hardly anything friendly or appealing about the site. I almost turned away and left before I began to see the beauty of it. You see, the character of the place in winter was more subdued. The clear, vivid impressions of summer were now the rounded lines and soft forms of winter's drifts and drooping, snow-laden trees. The flat portions of the site were gently rolling hummocks of snow. It was a campsite only because I knew that, under the snow, it held nice camping spots.

In summer, the impression of the site is immediate. One sees a well-worn path going from the water inland. Around the fire grate there are wood chips and twigs—the debris of many fires. The spots for tents look used, the grass and weeds around them flattened. You simply *know* it's a place frequently visited and enjoyed by your fellow creatures. Quite often, too, you find something they've forgotten. Tent stakes are the most common finds, but other times the find is big, a fishing tackle box, rod and reel, a ditty bag left hanging in a tree. The big finds trigger a feeling of sympathy for how the one who lost the item will feel when the loss is discovered. Put simply, a campsite in summer is full of evidence of people and feelings associated with people.

Disguised by winter, the campsite had almost fooled me. But the longer I looked the more evident it became—even with the signs well hidden, this was clearly a place partly sculpted by man. A short distance away a tree had been hacked by a foolish camper. A scrap of green parachute cord hung from a balsam branch. The faint line of a trail took off in two directions. The most used portions of the site were devoid of brush.

Indeed, even in winter, the nature of the campsite was clear. At first glance it may have looked like any other place along the shoreline, but it was more open, more cared for, more developed than any spot chosen at random. This campsite had been created over time. The obvious signs were few, but you knew it took people coming and going over the years to shape the place into something more useful than bare land.

I like that. Some people think of wilderness as a place devoid of signs of man. But that's not often the case. Wilderness can't help but show some signs of people having been there, having enjoyed it, having exploited it, or having respected it enough to fight for its preservation. There will always be some evidence of the relation between people and wilderness. Were we to rely on nature alone, the spots that would hold a seven-by-nine-foot tent would be few and far between, with no trails to connect them.

Man makes small changes in a wilderness setting. They are changes done by hand, and they blend with the character of the area. When a large, toppled tree is rolled into position near the fire so it can serve as a long bench, I don't feel outraged that something manmade has been left on the site. I like it because it beats sitting on the ground, and it makes use of something found at the site. Such a bench is part of the camping tradition in the area; besides, a natural log bench isn't very artificial. I do not like to see rickety tables nailed to trees, or other such junk. But within limits, rustic changes improve the character and utility of a site.

I'm not a purist or one to insist on "untrammeled nature." Nature gets plenty of wear and tear from storms, animals, insects, fire—and man. Deer and rabbits browse brush around a campsite, joining man in maintaining the clearing. When I look at a site, I see the work of animals and man together. The result of those changes is useful, beautiful, and blends with the environment.

Wilderness isn't a sterile place where nothing changes. Nature is dynamic, though most of its changes take place slowly, over long periods of time. It's like many people doing little things over many years to make a campsite, as opposed to someone on a bulldozer clearing the site in a day.

When I think of wild land, I think of balance. Within that environment things fit in and make sense. The marsh marigolds grow where high water will flood them in the spring, which is just what they like. The jackpine cling to rock or anchor in sandy soil where moisture is often scarce. Between these two extremes one finds the bulk of wild country vegetation, but each type searches out its own suitable niche, some, like the cedars, favoring damp humus, others, like thimbleberry, selecting more claylike soils. Every portion of the environment is suitable for some resident, the collection of all resident plants and animals providing a balanced whole.

I react in a similar way to other things. A farmhouse looks good in a farmland setting. Old warehouses look appropriate where they crowd a rail yard. If you put a thing in the wrong environment, it looks bad. It doesn't make sense anymore. If something is useful or functional, and appropriate for its environment, then it looks good—even beautiful. Beauty can tell us when something is right for its time and place.

Those were my thoughts as I viewed that campsite in winter. The nature of the situation seemed to prompt such ideas. I don't know if my train of thought would be the same if I viewed a city; I'm not sure I know how to comprehend an urban environment. But I suspect a city happens about the same way as a campsite does. Over time, people agree that such and such a place makes sense as a city. One area is perfect for factories and warehouses, another for houses, with the whole knit together by convenient transportation. That area, then, becomes a city. Other spots, decent enough but not excellent, become towns, while still other areas remain farmland. The mosaic of development reflects the character of the land.

The same is true of wilderness. On a particular lake, certain spots stand out as ideal places to camp. The ground is right, the view is good, natural resources make the spot appealing and it comes to be used as a campsite. Such primitive camping areas become established wilderness areas when enough people agree that the land should be left wild. When that happens, people are recognizing wild land for what it is—they are simply recognizing reality. Collective wisdom, then, dictates that the best use of that land is wilderness, where primitive camping is the norm.

Too often, unfortunately, some people regard wild land as a waste. They don't see any sense in having land that isn't developed or that doesn't produce. To their objections, I pose one question: "Why do you suppose this area has remained wild for so long?" I have to answer for them by saying, "This land didn't become a town or city or farm or orchard, so it must be that it isn't suited to such things. It stayed wild because that's what is right for the area. It can't be a waste for us to use wilderness land as wilderness, can it?"

Such arguments rise on logic. They fall on emotion. In this case, however, I think logic and emotion happen to coincide and I see no problem in leaving some areas alone. Each use of the land makes its own contribution. Cities provide what wild land cannot, and wild lands provide what cities lack. Though I confess to a bias for wilderness, (which I think is irreplaceable) I'm not hostile toward development or commerce.

I stayed on the campsite until I began to feel cold, then I skied back toward home. The day's adventure had given me exercise, then an uneasy view of a campsite, followed by a more reflective viewing of the site and of wilderness. I had, again, been a student of the land, letting it teach me by showing me what was there, so obvious. Somehow, the earth retains its power to show me reality. It gets through when other things fail. It even gets through when my mind's too crowded.

My skis carried me away, *kick–glide–kick–glide*, at a comfortable rhythm. It had been a good way to spend part of a day. I look forward to returning, winter or summer, to discover what nature will disclose next time.

Sled Dog

A crowd surrounds the starting area, the teams are being assembled, the cold air is full of urgent noises coming from man and beast. A sled dog race is about to begin. Sled dogs are primarily associated with the Arctic, and few images stand for the north as truly as does a dog team. There is a form of romance associated with dog teams and the lifestyle they've come to represent.

This doesn't mean that nothing has changed in the way dog teams are handled and trained. Indeed, the fastest dogs don't look anything like the "typical" sled dog we imagine. Fast dogs are built like runners; if anything, they resemble small Greyhounds.

Huskies and Samoyeds look like the sled dogs found in movies. They are big, have long coats and curled, bushy tails. As work dogs they combine speed with strength. A team of Husky dogs could handle a moderate freight load or provide fairly speedy transportation for people without the load.

The largest sled dogs are the Alaskan malamutes, which look like timber wolves (too much so in the minds of some people). The malamute is a freight-hauler built for strength rather than speed. These dogs were used to move large, heavy cargoes long distances in winter. They are, as well, very much outdoor dogs who are quite content staying outside in the cold.

Of the breeds mentioned, I'm most familiar with the malamute, so that's the breed I'm going to talk about. The name, malamute, I've been told, means "people." If that's the case, the name fits because malamutes and people have a long history together. Part of the "people" heritage in malamutes is that they like to talk. (No, they are not mute as the name seems to suggest, but they don't bark the way a normal dog does.) Malamutes are inclined to vocalize their feelings. They'll look you in the eye and *talk*; that's really the best word to describe it. Like wolves, they sing—part of a communicative social process of considerable complexity. Once in a while, though, a malamute will "woof" at something, to remind you he's a dog after all.

Malamutes are also funny. They are big, hardworking dogs, but they like to be silly. They are more than willing to bend their pride enough to engage in a romp. They are also a lot like cats. Malamutes like to pounce and leap, especially in tall grass or snow. They will pounce from spot to spot, almost like kittens, landing with their feet in a bunch. A malamute is in heaven when it can climb on something or gain a high perch. It will lie on one of these high places, then peer around like some great cat who rules the territory below.

The main characteristic of sled dogs, though, is that they love snow. Winter brings out the best in them. Malamutes are always ready to get going—to play, chase, burrow, or tow a sled, just as long as they can do it on snow. Winter seems to fill them with energy, and they look forward to a long, hard run. They like being sled dogs, and they throw themselves into the task. Partly, I'm sure, they do so to please their master, but they seem to have a natural enjoyment for hitting the trail.

On the negative side, sled dogs have a reputation for being fighters. If bored, overworked, or over-excited, they will get touchy. Who doesn't? Of course, some owners want more hyped-up dogs for racing, and those dogs can be hard to handle.

Before I bought my first malamute, I knew a little of what I was getting into. Unfortunately, I didn't know much about training malamutes—a problem made worse by the fact that I'd picked a so-so dog. I didn't make much progress working with her, so my experience duplicated that of her previous owners. In time, I lost interest and gave her away to a third set of owners. I had only learned that a malamute is not a pushover. My first attempt was a draw.

Fortunately, there are people in Hovland who raise malamutes. They thought my first dog had been too old to be trained (retrained?) properly, and they suggested I look at their next batch of pups. Well, you can imagine what happened. One of those pups worked his way into my heart, and there I was again with the old dream of "man and dog." I got the pick of the litter, a bold little guy with a black tip on his tail (the others had white tips).

For the first four months, the dog stayed where he was born, so he could be a puppy and learn with the other pups. Tim and Jan, the people who raised him, love dogs and have a natural sympathy for the animals. Their dogs are never meanly treated, which helps make them mellow animals. I'd describe Tim and Jan as being friends with their dogs, even though they are firm when firmness is needed. There is mutual respect between dogs and owners. I was thankful that they had agreed to look after the pup, which they named Canoe, after my love of canoeing and his love of water.

After I took Canoe home, I began to learn there was much give and take in training a dog. Often I want some behavior other than what I'm getting, but I have to discover if it's the dog not understanding or me not signaling clearly. A lot of patience and repetition is needed. I'm sure that I get as much training as the dog, so we learn together, almost as equals, because it's new to us both.

It surely is a slow process, though. Even with the preprogramming of breeding, it takes a long time before things are pulled into place. Regular, consistent effort is required to build the relationship and experience needed for man and dog to form a functional team. The mingling of human and dog destinies in the past must have been special. It makes me wonder—in the old sense of the word where "wonder" suggests awe. It's as if I can feel the centuries-old process of selective breeding, and with it the lives of many generations of dogs and the guiding hands of generations of breeders. My training of Canoe today is part of a process with roots reaching far back.

Recent evidence indicates that northern dogs were domesticated perhaps as early as 20,000 years ago. That's impressive. Man and dog have been together for a long time. That date, too, would make northern people world leaders in the trend to tame and integrate with wild animals, no small feat considering that they had to start from scratch in developing their training techniques. How long do you suppose it would take one of our better universities to turn a wild wolf pack into a harmonious dog team?

And so, Canoe and I are on a trail that stretches over centuries. Rich in meaning and the harvest of many winters, it is a trail of endurance and inspiration that brings us to this time and place. When I finish typing this, I'll go outside. Canoe will greet me with talk and body language. He's ready to go whenever I give the word. Together, we'll head into the bush for a healthy, happy run. While doing so, I'll be reminded of the trail of meaning that led me here. On that trail, I have learned that love, patience, and an attempt at understanding are as valid now as they were in the ancient past. In becoming part of a team with him I have learned much from Canoe; he's been an excellent instructor.

Tracking Wolves—Finding Predators

Several times during the past two weeks I've been roused from my sleep. During late winter, the wolves or coyotes (I don't know which) move closer to the lake and run past my house while in full cry. It's a crawly feeling to hear wild and powerful dogs so close to home. Their song and yipping are not pleasant when heard nearby. Awake and slightly irritated, I try to figure out what the wolves are up to so near my door, but before I can investigate, they are off. Their yips grow faint as the pack moves away. I roll over and slip back to sleep, like the drape that slips from my fingers as sleep releases my grip.

When morning comes I remember the wolves and, still in bed, flip aside the drape. A colder-than-usual night has left the panes frosted, so there is nothing to see but the growing brightness of a winter day. I roll from bed, and my feet tell me this day will begin with stoking the fire to drive back the chill that crept in during the dark. After I tend the wood stove, I'll fix my morning coffee.

Having my second cup at the table, my mind returns to the wolves. Memory of their calling voices is still powerful. There is a fascination in having wild creatures running free and advertising the fact. But I'm curious as to what they are, wolves or coyotes? My suspicion leans toward coyotes. Some of my neighbors, on the other hand, claim that the wolves are taking over and will kill all the wildlife and leave a wasteland.

The Eastern timber wolf is a protected animal with an interesting social structure and considerable stature. Wolves are also victims of mythology and bad reputations. In comparison, the coyote is more of a pest, often found in association with human development in an area. Some biologists have claimed that a hybrid-cross between household dogs and coyotes is the real culprit that has been breeding rapidly and tipping nature's balance. I'm not a biologist, but I like to see for myself what runs past my house on winter nights.

Having other things to do first, I was on snowshoes shortly after noon. In March the snow is sometimes crusty and solid enough that you think you can do without snowshoes—that is, until you try it. Snowshoes over crusty snow, though, makes for fast travel. In no time I located tracks right behind the woodshed. The tracks include deer impressions and doglike prints. I follow them going parallel to the lake for a half-mile before they turn north, away from the open shoreline and heading into denser forest.

I follow the narrow track-line the deer have made over an entire winter. A deer trail is like a V-shaped valley formed as their small hooves sink deep and define a narrow pathway. Running in the track-line and on either side are doglike prints, seemingly in pursuit. The dog tracks are bigger than those of most dogs, and dogs don't form packs of animals all so much the same size. So, I know I'm trailing wolves or coyotes, but I am not able to tell which from the tracks alone. The size, however, doesn't seem large enough to be Eastern timber wolf tracks, which are 4 inches long, like those of a malamute. The tracks I'm following are only slightly longer than average dog prints, perhaps 2½ or 3 inches at most.

I'm not learning much about my nighttime visitors, but I follow the tracks farther in the hope of coming across a solid clue. Another twenty minutes brings me to a logged-over clearing, approximately two miles from my house.

As I enter the clearing, I feel the brightness all around. It hurts my eyes, and I wish the trail had stayed in the shaded forest. My eyes stinging and watering, I stay with the tracks, which are now running northwest along a path that has me struggling up hill. The bright light makes me squint and sweat runs down my face and around my eyes, which is probably why three deer are able to take me by surprise. They rise from their bedding spots in a clump of low balsam fir. One snorts as the trio bounds away to the east, tail flags flying. Apparently those three eluded the pack last night. So, there's a balance, after all, even though I had assumed that wolves had a strong advantage on snow and could kill at will. These deer were confident enough to bed down next to the path the wolves had so recently taken.

The deer are long gone while I'm still catching my breath. The logging clearing provides new growth (browse) for deer, and it must attract them, judging from the many deer tracks that crisscross through the clearing and branch out from the main line of tracks. Following the main track, I can see places all along the way where next spring's buds have been nibbled off by hungry deer.

At the top of the clearing, the pattern changes. There, I enter new terrain of high, rocky ridges covered with jackpine. Standing on a crest, I can see the line of deer tracks as it runs along the edge of the jackpine ridge. Jackpines offer little browse for deer, so they avoid it, staying in the mixed forest of the lower slopes. The wolves, however, depart from the deer trail here. A wide path of doglike prints heads into the ridges, with their pine cover and elevated views.

After a short pause, I decide to follow the wolf trail higher in the hope that I may yet come across a solid clue. Climbing, I wonder why the wolves went this way, away from the deer country below. Then it hits me. Up here the going is easy. The windswept ridges run for miles and miles, and from these ridges the predators can drop down on a pocket of deer almost at will. So, even just following their route has shown me more about these animals, who hunt over a wide area. That explains why I don't hear them every night. Such a hunting tactic makes me think I must be tracking wolves rather than coyotes, but I still don't know which. Six miles from home, I give up the chase, seemingly no closer to an answer than when I started.

Walking back, I feel let down. I've not come up with anything concrete, only impressions and more observation. In time, this day may make a contribution, but for now it seems little more than good exercise obtained during a futile investigation attempt.

The cold seems to bite more sharply. My mood is in keeping with the time of day—the shadows are getting longer and my snowshoes creak louder as the temperature starts to drop. At the logging clearing, I stop again to catch my breath. The wind is picking up. Grains of snow skitter over the crusted clearing and whirl around like little dust-devils made of snow. I wonder about the deer that rely on this clearing, and I wonder about the predators that depend on deer and other herbivores. I really want to know more, so I can help make the right decisions for this beautiful, challenging land and its wild inhabitants. As I stand in the clearing I am reminded of another cause for concern. I am reminded of the snow. I wonder what it will do to all of this.

The innocent, driven snow contains a serious and growing threat. It is acid rain in storage—a winter's worth of accumulated corrosives. Acid rain and acid snow will, in time, have an impact on the forest by attacking tender, new growth—growth that is needed by browsing animals, and needed for the forest to survive. When acid rain acidifies the soil, growth is stunted and blunted. Where does that leave our wildlife? Homeless and foodless, that's where.

When the acid showers of April mingle with the melting drifts of November to March, we don't get May flowers, we get an acid flush. Unleashed over a short period of time and undiluted by mixing with standing bodies of water, our acid flush is just in time to sterilize fish and frog eggs while it stunts the growth of aquatic plants.

If acid rain and acid snow go unchecked, the result will be a northern desert. The green won't die all at once; the older, sturdier trees will remain, but new growth will become rarer and rarer. The lakes won't stop containing fish in a season or two; mature fish will struggle along, surviving on the few minnows and insects that lived through the acid bath. The destruction will happen slowly, but it *will* happen.

It sounds serious, because it *is* serious. The Ph scale doesn't lie, and the scale shows a steady trend toward more and more acid in our sensitive northern environment. Slowing the rate of acidification will help, but the only cure is to keep acid rain out of delicate ecosystems by demanding strict air and water standards.

The innocent snow whirling in the clearing as I head for home is both symbol and omen. Snow is a symbol of purity. Snow stands as winter's legacy of water formed into an earth-protecting blanket. The omen is that winter's legacy is severely tainted by our urbanized-industrialized society, and if it continues to be contaminated, then all this day's topics won't matter. The deer won't browse and the wolves won't howl in an environment sterilized dead by acid. In our concern for predators and their control, we can now look at the sky where a new predator rides, mouth agape. Drop our wildlife heritage into the acid maw and watch it dissolve. Where acid rain is on the prowl, nothing else will survive. Acid rain, the ultimate predator, will consume it all.

Through the Ice

This is a story I tell on myself. It's about a blunder and how easy it was to make.

It happened several years ago, when my interest in winter camping was being renewed. I was game for almost any experience in the bush, so when friends suggested to trek to a remote shack, I agreed. Those old cabins, now mostly gone, were once an important part of winter survival for those who worked in the woods most of the year. Our plan called for removing snow from the roof and doing a few minor repairs to keep the place from falling apart.

Our trip in was pleasant. It was a good day for snowshoeing, and the four of us took turns breaking trail. A few times we'd hit air pockets, where the snow was mounded over fine branches and weeds. When you got over a pocket, the snow would suddenly collapse, and the trail would sink several feet into the newly formed hole. That's a somewhat common hazard on brushy trails, but most of the going was good, and it was just cold enough for the hard work of opening trail.

When we got to the Arrow River, just above a small set of rapids, the water was frozen—just like a road. So, we turned onto the river for the last leg of our trip. On the way, we passed a spot where two moose had fought. The area was heavily trampled, and there were blood speckles and a small antler that had been broken off in the fight.

While going about the day's activity, I began to think about returning for another trip. The spot above the rapids was nice for camping, and it was part of some territory I'm quite fond of. Before the day was over I talked to one of my companions and we agreed to return the following weekend to do some camping and exploring. With the fresh trail we'd just made, we figured we'd have a good route for towing in our camping gear.

The summer before, I had been in Canada where I bought a book on northern winter survival. That book referred to the frozen rivers of the north as *natural highways*. I had always been leery of river travel, but the idea was appealing. A frozen river is flat and easy to follow. So, part of my plan for the coming weekend was to free-ski upriver and explore areas hard to travel in summer. My fear of ice formed over moving water had been safely put to rest by the book I'd read.

Fortunately, when the weekend came no fresh snow had fallen, and the trail was still good. The preceding six days, however, had been somewhat milder. That's not too unusual, and such weather forms a tough crust on the snow, so I didn't see any need to change our travel plans.

We had little trouble reaching the river, though along the way we stopped often to make minor changes in the towing rig. It was a beautifully bright winter day, the trail was good, and we felt no pressure. As I recall, we got to the campsite above the rapids around 1:00 in the afternoon.

Once we arrived, we unloaded the toboggan. We had put off having lunch until reaching the site, where we intended to sit down and eat. However, I wanted to get as much done as possible. I had packed a metal can with paper, pencils, matches, candles, and other supplies to leave in the shack for "emergencies." The shack wasn't far away and it seemed like a good idea to drop the stuff off. That would get one chore out of the way and leave the next day free for exploring. So, we grabbed the lunch and the can and snowshoed to the river.

The river looked different. There was more open water above the rapids, and the ice cover looked darker in spots. It didn't look sound. However, it had been solid as rock the weekend before, and I didn't think the ice situation was serious. The ice had supported two huge moose, hadn't it? I discarded the evidence of my eyes in favor of the book I'd read, which had assured me that frozen rivers were the winter highways of the north.

I was in the lead, and my sense of caution kept me close to shore. I assumed the current was slower along shore, and that the worst ice would be near the rapids, where the water started to speed up. The path I had taken looked fine. There was no sign of weakness in the ice. As we got farther from the rapids, the ice looked better, and I felt more relaxed as I continued moving along.

In mid-stride, I felt myself sink, and then I was entering the water. The ice had collapsed under me, forming a bowl of black water. As I went down I tried to fall to one side in the hope of catching firmer ice before I went under. That worked! I ended up with the upper part of my chest on solid ice, but I was still three-quarters in the water. I can tell you one thing: It's impossible to swim while wearing snowshoes and winter clothing. Wet, I weighed a great deal. I kicked my legs and tried to keep pulling forward, all the while hoping the ice would hold.

There's no need to explain what went through my head. My main thought was, "This is IT!" Strangely, once I made a little progress out, I was concerned about the fate of my companion. I kept looking back to see if he was safe. I'd rather have only one of us go, if that was to be the case.

I continued to kick and work my way out. The worst part was getting the snowshoes out of the hole; they kept catching on the ice. But I continued crawling forward and managed to hold them clear. During this time, too, I think my partner and I were hollering back and forth, but most of my attention went into crawling ahead. Even free of the hole, I continued to crawl until I reached the safety of the riverbank.

After I reached the bank, *then* I stood up. With numb-curiosity, I looked back at the hole I'd crawled from. That's when it started to hit me. Crawling along on the snow had blotted some water from me, but I was cold, shaking from that as well as from fear. I knew the situation was serious, but I didn't feel much physical distress. My ability to feel was apparently damped down, and I wasn't entirely rational. I remember thinking, "That's how close I came," as I looked at the hole.

By then my companion had joined me on the bank, but in all honesty, I don't remember our conversation. I assume we tried to decide what to do, while I stood there and shook. The possibility of getting me dried out and warm back at the campsite was dim. It was doubtful I'd last long enough, as I was, to walk back to the truck. The best bet was to get to the shack and build a fire. The shack, unfortunately, was across the river, and I had no desire to go anywhere near the river. My partner and I talked over the options, but to this day I'm foggy about the details.

Even at the time I knew one thing—I would die of exposure if I didn't get warmed up and dry. And, although the river repelled me, crossing it seemed no worse than dying of exposure where I was. Without taking action I'd die standing right there, so a strange kind of logic told me to try to reach the shack with its wood stove. As I took a few steps on the riverbank, I saw that my clothes were beginning to freeze. That gave me a sense of urgency, and I moved as quickly as I could to a point directly across the river from where the shack lay hidden in the fir trees.

Bravely saying that I would try to cross the river first since I was already wet was one thing. Actually putting a foot back on the ice after having just gone through was something else. I had to pause. Actually, I was scared. To give myself courage, I found a dead, standing aspen pole nearby. Less than six inches in diameter and perhaps twelve or fifteen feet long, the pole broke near the base. It would give me something to hang on to if the ice gave way again.

I held my pole horizontal at the center and ventured onto the ice. I wanted to go quickly but without running, so I did a fast shuffle on my snowshoes. When I reached the other side, my friend followed. It was a relief to be across, and we went right to the shack.

I can't tell you how good that rundown old building looked. We got a fire going in the stove, which was so decrepit and leaky that it filled the cabin with a smoky pall. But it felt awfully good, even with the choking smoke, to be semi-secure after a close call. The shack was as primitive as a place could be, but it was many times better than trying to dry clothing around an outside fire. Considering all the desolate places I've been in the bush, this was a darn convenient spot to have a serious mishap. If it was more than luck, then it must have been providence.

My mind and body were still reacting as I dried clothes, and I had to keep reminding myself this was real. A shock like the one I'd had doesn't just go away. The combined physical and emotional drain leaves a person punchy, and my moods were bouncing from fear to joy. However, after several hours of drying clothes, I had become somewhat calmer. I was no longer shaking, and was dry enough to travel. I felt inclined to stay, possibly forever, in the shack, but food, camping gear, and all my spare clothes were back at the campsite.

Getting dry and stabilizing my body had been my first major concern. Now I was faced with another problem—the river had to be crossed *again*. The thought of getting wet another time was intolerable. Having already come across the river was obvious proof that it could be done, but I had to swallow hard to do it once more. Again, I went first, my aspen pole giving me courage. My friend joined me soon after I reached the other side, and we made tracks to the campsite.

The light was starting to go and the cold was becoming more penetratingly obvious. We didn't waste any time. As soon as we reached our site, I changed into my spare boot liners. Then, because we were getting a late start, I threw myself into the work, partly from nerves and partly to keep warm. Fortunately, the two of us were experienced enough to be able to put up a good camp in short order.

In an hour we were getting ready to eat a hot meal. While our food warmed, we talked. I learned from my partner how his moods had bounded wildly up and down as he reacted to what had happened to me. Simply being an "observer" had left him feeling exhausted. The day's events had placed a huge strain on both of us, and I realized that it was lucky for me he'd been along and was such a reliable fellow. I recall him saying that he was relieved to have this experience behind us, but for me, the biggest relief was that I did not have to go back on the river.

At the time, I realized how lucky I had been. Now, I feel darn thankful. There is a distinction there, but I won't dwell on it. Shortly after the incident, I tried to put it out of mind. I didn't want to tell anyone what a fool I had been. I was embarrassed. I didn't think I had a big ego, but it was too big to admit to a mistake on my part. I blamed the ice.

As you might guess, my evaluation of the incident has changed. My accident taught me a few things, though it took time to sort them out. The first step was to stop keeping what had happened a secret. As a secret, it wasn't doing me or anyone else any good. I had acted fairly well at the time, but my attitude toward the affair afterward was far from solid or constructive. The fact that I should have known better did not alter the reality of what had happened. I had lots of junk to toss aside in order to make use of the situation. I had to deal with it realistically, and I now realize the following things:

The safety of ice over moving water is always questionable. It only takes one weak spot to dump you. There is simply no adequate way to identify all the weak spots. I'll stick to the riverbanks for travel, thank you, and leave the river for the fish.

No plan should preclude the possibility of a mishap. Accidents can and will happen. A good plan minimizes your chances for misfortune, but beyond that, it also provides options for dealing with an accident.

The value of being over-prepared and of carrying spare supplies is obvious. In my case, they made the difference between salvaging part of the weekend and having to give up. Also, spares add a degree of security to any decisions that must be made, particularly in an emergency.

It is best to know the area through which you're traveling, have good trails, and have adequate camping skills. All of these provide some opportunity to rebound. Had I broken through the ice in strange territory toward the end of a tough day, my story would have been much different.

In winter, little problems can be serious. Even if just one of your boots gets soaked, it still represents a significant loss. A good plan will take into account the potential gravity of minor problems.

Solo camping provides the least potential for recovery. Pair camping is better, but the strain on two people is quite large. A larger group has a greater safety factor in the event of a crisis. Remember that everyone is affected in such a situation. At least two of the campers in a group should be experienced and capable.

Respect winter. Feelings of fear are often realistic warnings. We seldom feel fear for *no* reason. Experienced campers, in particular, run the risk of ignoring fear and becoming overconfident. Beginning campers may be too fearful. The path between these two extremes forms a realistic relationship between the camper and the winter environment.

Exercising wisdom, caution, and understanding is essential to survival during a crisis. Never forget how easily the elements can overpower you. I lived through a narrow escape, but it was the work of another power that taught me survival.

Winter Night

Nathaniel Hawthorne, in his preface to *The Scarlet Letter*, wrote about the effect of moonlight on the interior of a room. The pale light changed the aspect of things, and Hawthorne found that the faint light reminded him of the dim past. His observation hit upon a striking reality. The world under moonlight seems to be in reversal. It is more like being in a photographic negative than in the world to which we are accustomed. Hawthorne wrote before photography was invented, but he saw in moonlight an additional perspective.

You can experience this phenomenon of altered perspective by going out for a night ski tour. A short tour is best, just enough to stretch the muscles and to see what's around. It takes a while for the eyes to become accustomed to dim light, but once they have, it's sufficient for careful touring. I'd suggest, as well, that you follow trails you're familiar with at a pace that won't leave you soaking wet.

A little moonlight goes a long way. The snow-covered ground is reflective, so it seems the light is rising from the earth. The trail you follow will be dappled in light and shadow, but not the familiar lights and darks of daylight. Moonlight coming through the trees creates a patterned lacework that forms a complex design. In places, the light will accent a particular spot. It may be just a branch with a few leaves still clinging, but it will stand out with unusual clarity, almost in isolation. Such clear emblems sometimes have a special meaning, as well—they are familiar landmarks in the altered landscape disclosed under a cold-glowing winter moon.

In daylight a trail is an obvious path. In winter moonlight, a trail is a close, mysterious way. Visibility is good, but it is limited to what is near at hand. A trail reveals itself only as you move along. A shadow will block the way until you reach it and pass through. Immediate surroundings are the only things seen in detail. Distance is perceived in a new way—according to what is just ahead. Conditions keep focus close at hand, and even as one moves toward them, far-off hills or a line of trees are indistinct shapes that seem remote in relation to the more intimate impressions that surround the skier.

From a high trail you can see through the trees to the lake below, the valley-bounded lake, like a bright, solid cloud against the black hills. You can trace the river, like a silver pathway unshadowed by the surrounding forest. There is grandeur in the views along a scenic trail. It is a spectacle of beauty to see the land in the garb of winter light. But, always, you return to the enclosed space of the forested path. There you travel in confined territory, where a dark shadow blocks the way until you reach it, enter it, and find it has disappeared and has become more forest-surrounded trail.

Windigo

The Ojibway people have a legend about the Windigo, an evil spirit that revealed itself most often in winter. Native people were split into smaller groups during the winter season, making it a period of high vulnerability. If conditions were poor, hunting bad, or sickness prevalent, the Windigo spirit could exercise a powerful influence.

The Windigo spirit, in a person, placed individual survival above that of anyone else. A Windigo is selfishness run wild. At its peak form, the Windigo led to cannibalism, especially during times of starvation. Once a person had become a cannibal, he went crazy and could not live without consuming more and more human lives. Windigo spirits, living in their host-victims, were thought to roam the forest like wild men searching for new human prey. The Windigo spirit found its opportunity by moving into a person with a weak, selfish, or fearful personality, thus turning the unfortunate individual into a dreadful, living Windigo.

The names of some of our lakes, like Windigo Lake, Cannibal Lake, Ghost, Haunted, or Black Lakes, reflect these tales. Places where cannibalism had taken place were shunned, because it was believed that the evil spirit still dwelt there.

Selfishness run wild was a threat to the people's base of survival—it was what they feared most. About any selfish behavior, the Indian people were inclined to say: "It must be terrible to feel that way." Stories about Windigo spirits reflect a social danger that was most apparent in winter, when life was difficult. If the bonds of love and cooperation were broken by the selfish concerns of an individual, the universe of the people was ruptured. The living society, then, had to maintain the values that made them a people rather than a collection of hostile factions. The occurrence of a Windigo (in fact or legend) was a stern reminder of what could happen if the way of peace among people was neglected.

In reading about modern expeditions, the tale is often the same. Fragmentation, hostility, anger, and defensiveness are all little Windigo acts. Native people certainly knew enough about life in the bush, under pressure, to identify correctly the nature of enemy.

I mention this Indian legend because it helps to impart an important lesson. Life then was just as we know it today, not some ideal, simple, carefree existence. Facing rough times together was tolerable as long as the bonds of cooperation were unbroken.

Any situation that places stress on mind and body can be destructive. The danger of Windigo thinking and behavior still exists. The Indian reaction to that danger was to stress reconciliation and social unity. Part of the unity came through legend. Knowing about the dangers of a Windigo spirit was one way to be warned and to act otherwise. Legends didn't function to frighten people. They were there to instruct—to point out obvious social truths.

I think the camping tradition of Native Americans offers valuable insight into living with people. The Indians were experts at living together. They sought harmony with nature and with one another. Skill in hunting, a good harvest, adequate preparation, and other practical concerns were, perhaps, not as crucial to survival as was maintaining peace.

It is difficult to take legend from one people and pass it along in useful form to people in a different time, who may well dismiss it as superstition. At best, one catches the spirit of the legend, though that is sometimes sufficient. In any case, the spirit of past days transcends, both in meaning and importance, the few pieces of physical evidence and assorted tales left behind by an earlier culture.

When civilized people look at primitive people, they see what the others lack in terms of material goods. Yet primitive societies were fully functional on all levels, material and social. The civilized view suggests that primitives were unhappy and suffered from a lack of material comfort or success. Native culture, however, shows that the opposite was true. Having little (as we view it), they appreciated what they had and were generous with it. The "civilized" notion that poverty breeds misery and mean-spirited behavior is the viewpoint of a materialistic people who think they describe another society, when they are in fact reflecting their own preoccupation with material culture. Civilization's concept of Native society was formed by looking in a mirror.

The point of this, partly, is that the Windigo legend is not a superstition. It is a way of describing unsocial human behavior and questionable personality traits gone unchecked. The Indian people knew what the legend meant, it was the civilized folks who had trouble figuring it out. Fortunately, we can still benefit from past experience, even experience first presented to us in a distorted way. Re-examining legend gives us something in common with those who lived here before us, because legend deals with a common concern—namely, that of being human.

Sauna

At the end of a day on snowshoes, the prospect of an hour or two in a steamy, soothing sauna is most welcome. My sauna, or bathhouse as it was once called, is the hot-humid type. It was here when I bought the property, and I've simply added to its more-than-ample basic form.

For some reason, I think of taking a sauna as a winter activity. It was the winter season, too, which rekindled my interest in the sauna after I'd lost the habit of using it. A sauna doesn't, however, have a seasonal limit, and can be enjoyed year-round.

Come to think of it, the word sauna is an all-round word. The same word describes both the building and the bath taken in it. In some part of the north country, particularly where Finnish people have settled, you might hear, "Come and sauna," which means, "Come and join us in the sauna for a sauna and for the shared experience." *Sauna*, then, means a building, a bath, a kind of human interaction.

Of the three meanings, the third is the most interesting. Sometimes when I mention "interaction in the sauna," I see a smutty smirk or two. I'd be the last to deny that saunas have been used for lusty pleasures, but that's not my focus here.

To explain interaction, let me list some of the historic uses the sauna has been put to. As a clean, warm building, the sauna was often used for giving birth. For family care, the heated sauna made laundering and hygiene possible. Steamed herbs were part of a therapeutic bath session where a form of folk medicine was practiced. Like shared meals, washing with others in the sauna was a healthy-human practice.

Of the above uses, I've heard frequent speculation about the health role of the sauna. Some claim that healing vapors are released in old-time saunas or sweat lodges, where birch bark roofs are exposed to the steamy heat generated when water is poured over fire-heated rock. Others claim that a hot sauna is like an artifical fever that cleans and purges the body of germs, killing them with heat. In the future, I hope the health contribution of the sauna will be adequately studied.

To an American, the traditional family sauna is startling because of its group nudity of both sexes. We are not accustomed to much nudity, even in the confines of our athletic or health clubs among members of the same sex. The casual nudity of family saunas is not our style.

Having said that, I'm forced to recognize our modern association of nudity with sexual opportunity. In an earlier day, nudity was not a moral issue at all. It was, rather, a condition that went along with being undressed to bathe, change clothing, swim, or even perform certain tasks. In our modern society, however, nudity is compromising and suggestive of vulnerability —unfortunate associations. Today we are lucky if we can view being naked as an un-loaded situation. We have difficulty seeing nakedness for what it is—a form of honesty, which neither teases nor hides.

The Indian people of the north had their version of the sauna, called the sweat lodge. Built like a small wigwam and holding only a few people, the sweat lodge used heated rocks and water, just like the sauna. The steam was sometimes enhanced in its qualities by the addition of herbs and grasses over the hot rocks. Stripped to the skin, a person in a sweat lodge was purified and renewed. A similar lodge was used for healing rites. All sweat lodge rites were closely linked to spiritual growth.

I've found it ironic that two groups from cold winter areas would both develop a love for a hot, steamy bath. Could it be that frigid February days inspire a yearning for tropical conditions? Perhaps it's just that an excess of heat can make a northern resident feel secure from the chill, at least for a while, though after a long sauna one is most often glad for the chilly air.

So, why does a freezing day inspire me to build a fire in the sauna stove? I don't know. But I know I enjoy my sauna and the tradition it represents.

Wigwam

(Author's Note: When first written, the Wigwam piece was based on information available from historic sources. Recent archaeological evidence, however, begins to suggest that the wigwam represents only one form of Native shelter, there having been many other adaptations over the preceeding ten thousand years, the period of post-glacial human history in the north country.)

The camping tradition would seem to begin with skin tents as portable shelters. To a degree that is true. Skin tents were portable, but they were often used on permanent sites, with a fixed framework of rock or wood. Portable housing is related to camping, but the camping tradition was different in the past because it had a different purpose.

The wigwam, frequently associated with life in the north country, allows us to glimpse conditions of winter living conducted in a simple shelter. The wigwam was a form of portable shelter, but it was not quickly moved or reset. It was, after all, large enough to house an extended family and stores of supplies. A common dimension for a wigwam, which is shaped like a Quonset hut, is about 15 feet long by 12 feet wide. However, it's reasonable to assume that the size of the structure depended on family requirements. Large family groups may have had a number of wigwams located together in a basic design resembling modular housing. A large single unit could be built by extending the length, making a sort of wigwam long house, or a number of smaller standard units could be used where the terrain lacked sufficient building space on the same level.

Regardless of the exact details of organization, the wigwam provided shelter and storage for groups with members of all ages, from infant to elderly. The design had to be functional; for centuries it provided substantial shelter for the preservation of human life.

Wigwams were moved on a seasonal basis to take advantage of hunting and gathering opportunities. A framework of bent poles was prepared at each new site, while on previously used sites the existing frames would be repaired or altered to be used again. The covering, rolls of birch bark for the roof and reed mats for the walls, was prepared along traditional dimensions. Thus, the ultimate size of the wigwam depended on the number of rolls available. In this, too, there is a modular approach around a basic design, similar to our use today of standard sizes in building materials.

Preparation of the covering was tied to the seasons. Bark was best secured in early summer while it was still flexible. Reed mats were prepared later in the season. It is likely that these units lasted for years. Single rolls would be replaced as needed, and it was seldom that the entire covering had to be replaced. These rolls, which were bulky but not heavy, were the main ingredient that had to be moved from site to site.

The pole framework could not be secured once the ground froze, so winter housing had to be established before that time. In late summer and fall, small temporary shelters in the hunting area would be established. Thus, the winter season saw a main cluster of wigwams used by family groupings, and smaller outposts used for overnight stays by hunters too far from the main cluster to return the same day. This multiple housing approach provided a degree of safety and back-up housing. Fire in a wigwam could destroy it quickly, so having a number of wigwams in an area provided needed housing if one burned. The wigwam represented a carefully devised system for living that took shape along seasonal patterns calling for a considerable amount of preplanning.

A closer look at the wigwam in winter offers testimony to its practicality. In essence, it provided everything a modern house provides. Panels of sewn skins or densely woven reed mats lined the inner walls to a height of four feet. This gave a sitting and sleeping area that was draft free inside, while utilizing the hollow space between walls and liner to provide enough air flow to remove smoke.

The wigwam even had central heating. Light and heat came from a small central fire. Smoke left the wigwam through vents located high on both ends. To prevent spoilage, some foods were hung in the upper part of the wigwam, where they would be smoked. Standing in the wigwam was kept to a minimum because of the smoke, but the lower four feet were relatively smoke free due to the liner. One end of the wigwam might be reserved for storage. Seating and sleeping places were located on platforms of insulating boughs that ran along the walls and exposed the occupants to equal shares of radiant heat from the fire.

Wigwam living was compact but cozy. The modern reader will probably think the interior was too smoky for comfort. It was not. The liner in a wigwam functioned exactly as the dew liner in a tipi, a model of efficient, portable housing. Keep in mind that in Europe during the same period, most peasant cottages were without chimneys. Rural European housing got rid of smoke exactly as the Indians did, through vents in the gables or roof. The fireplace we think of as synonomous with early America was a compromise innovation, not suited to extreme cold and not found in housing for the poor. Chimneys did not become common on homes until comparatively recent years, when affordable stoves were made of ceramic or metal. For its time, the wigwam provided excellent accommodation for living in a harsh climate. The Native American population enjoyed a higher standard of sanitation and efficiency than people who lived in the slums of London.

The shape of the wigwam was well suited to winter, shedding snow easily and providing ample wall space for sitting and sleeping platforms. The compactness of the wigwam made it easy to heat in severe cold. In such a small area, even the body heat of the occupants raised the temperature inside.

The wigwam was a product of a highly adapted people and their lifestyle.

The full nature of that lifestyle is something we have yet to realize. It grew under demanding conditions and reflects humanity at its practical best. It was a way of living that holds worthwhile lessons for us, even though many years have passed since wigwams dotted the winter landscape.

Cabin-House

"Outside, a winter storm thumps the side of my house like a pillowed fist. The electricity was knocked out two hours ago, so I am sitting at the kitchen table, writing in the small circle of light cast by a glass kerosene lamp that came with the place. Tomorrow when it's light, I'll go out to find drifts formed of wind-driven snow hurled across Lake Superior. Tomorrow there will be shoveling to do and a snow-decorated house to admire. But for now, I'm snug and content. My airtight Ashley stove creaks in the contest between its self-contained heat and cold gusts trying to invade it through the chimney. The house is cozy—its construction took into account nights and storms like this. I have prepared for such conditions so that I might face them in peace."

I wrote the above paragraph during a winter storm, the winter season being the one that causes me to most appreciate my house. With it, I am able to do more than survive. The house provides an environment where I can be productive, where I can write. So, this piece, like many of the others in this section, is one inspired by, but not exclusively about, winter. The lessons of my cabin-house are most clear when set against the demands of winter, but they are useful for all the seasons.

I bought the property and cabin more than a dozen years ago. I was drawn back to Hovland, where as a boy I was first exposed to the north country on family vacations and fishing excursions on the border lakes. It was one of those fortunate "coincidences" that enabled me to find a teaching job here, where I wanted to live. It was like a dream. I had a job and a cabin in the woods on the north shore of Lake Superior.

I knew the cabin needed work, but other people (including an elderly widow) had lived in it year-round, so I figured I could too. The main room was 16 feet by 16 feet. It was constructed of hewn logs with dovetail corners. Around three sides of the cabin, lean-to additions had been added for kitchen, bath, bedroom, and porch. There was another, loft-style bedroom above the main room. The cabin was small but functional. I really liked it, so much so that after I first moved in, I spent many hours simply looking at it and feeling content.

When fall came, I had to disconnect and drain the running water. The water, which came from the lake, was not winterized. However, it promised to be a simple enough matter to haul water and keep enough on hand for my use. It was inconvenient, but I could rough it; a relatively easy task for someone without a family. Eventually, I hoped to winterize the water system to have running water all year.

My first warning that things might not be so simple came after Christmas. I had gone up to the Iron Range to visit my parents, and during that time we had a cold snap. The oil burner in the cabin had been left on medium, but when I walked into the cabin after my absence the interior felt chilly. The oil burner was functioning, but the heat was being lost.

I started to look the situation over. It wasn't good. All the canned items in the kitchen cupboards were frozen solid. It was quite a mess, and for the rest of the winter I had to leave the cupboards partly open so the contents wouldn't freeze. In the bathroom, a solid block of ice had formed in the toilet bowl. Flushing was impossible, and the toilet was cracked, creating an unexpected replacement expense. When I sat down in the living room to consider this new state of affairs, I had to do so while resting my feet on a chair in order to keep them warm. Even with the heat turned up, the floor of the cabin was cold and drafty, as if a miniature arctic weather system raged at floor level.

I dug in, so to speak, and made my stand. It was me against the elements, right inside the cabin. As I look back on it, a good portion of my winter camping experience came *in* the cabin. I closed off rooms so I wouldn't have to heat them. It was more comfortable in the house when the wood stove was burning, but I had to be gone during the day and I returned home to a chilly cabin. I'd rekindle a fire and have it burning hot by the time I had to retire for the night, thus enjoying only a short period of comfort indoors. The only encouraging thing was the mice—the cold brought them in, so apparently my meager existence was appealing to some form of life.

Thoreau's comments about essential livng took on vivid meaning as I settled in to battle the invading cold. I had to make adjustments to those pressing external forces. Fortunately, the mice were suckers for a Victor trap prepared with peanut butter, so the uninvited guests were soon under control. Having closed off the lower bedroom, I moved to the loft. Heat rises, so the loft was the warmest room in the cabin. I thought my most urgent troubles to be at an end.

One night in February I woke to the smell of smoke. Panicked by the prospect of fire, I scrambled for the upstairs door. As soon as I opened it, smoke poured into the bedroom, and I heard a muffled *whump* come from downstairs. Afraid of what I'd find, I searched from room to room. I found no fire, but there was lots of smoke, oily-smelling smoke. A winter storm had become more intense since I'd retired, and I soon discovered what was happening. A howling gust of wind would blow down the chimney, extinguishing the oil burner, which would then relight with a *whump* and an impressive belch of sooty smoke.

That went on all night. There I was in a hard-to-heat cabin with doors and windows open during a winter storm in order to let the smoke out. The sooty smoke had covered everything with an oily, black film. Somehow I managed to get to my job the next day without looking like a coal miner, but the work of cleaning the cabin took days.

By the time spring arrived, I knew I had to make changes before the next winter. It made no sense to winterize the water system with the cabin the way it was. And I wanted to do something about a new source of heat. I was through with that soot-belching oil burner.

So, I came up with a plan. I could not afford to rebuild the entire place in one season, so I decided to make improvements in stages. The worst area seemed to be the north addition, which contained a bedroom and bath. The west side of the house would be next. The east side, which included the kitchen, would come after that, while the upstairs loft would be last.

All in all, it looked like I had four or five years of work ahead of me. However, as soon as I started to dig into the first phase, I could see it was building up to be much more than I had anticipated. The north addition was impossible to repair and had to be torn down to the ground. A basement crawl area had to be dug, footings poured, a cement block wall built over the footings—*then*, I could start rebuilding the rooms I'd lost. I learned that on an old house, remodeling is often reconstruction. The first phase of the job took most of the summer and fall.

I had help from friends, and I needed it because the project required more than I had to give. When building, you only get one convenient chance to do it right. So, the old wiring, consisting of two circuits, had to go; it was replaced by a circuit breaker system. The wiring had to be done before the insulation could be added. The project was a full-size puzzle in three dimensions.

My university training had not included carpentry and electrical repair. I was nearly useless if I just tried to read about some skill. But once someone showed me what do to, and after I had a chance to apply my knowledge, I usually got a grasp of it. To my academic mind it came as a shock to discover I had to learn basic skills just like everyone else. However, I didn't have time to ponder my shortcomings. There was too much to get done. The first cold blast arrived the night I put in the last of the insulation. I'd just made it, but I had run out of money at that point and only had unfinished rooms to show for my efforts. The oil burner had been replaced, though, and I had a new gas furnace to keep me warm. I felt as if I'd made real progress.

My feeling of progress diminshed as winter grew in intensity. The new, insulated rooms on the cabin took care of only 25 percent of the problem. The place was still darn cold and drafty. I started to devise plans to deal with each of the remaining parts of the cabin. My priorities reflected the failings of the existing structure. The cabin lacked insulation, good windows, and solid doors, so these things were put high on my list. I figured that as long as it was a small place, I could take my time and do it right. The cabin had rustic character, which I wanted to keep. But I wanted to use good materials and have something worth the effort when it was done.

It turned out to be more than a four- or five-year project. Ten years is more accurate, and it is still not complete, though it is virtually entire and quite functional.

As my work progressed, I kept having skirmishes with nature. After I got rid of the mice by installing a full foundation, I had to find where the shrews were getting in and fight them off. During another summer the carpenter ants took a crack at the kitchen. The last enemy was a "flock" of bats that hung in the gables and eaves. Ordinarily they stayed outside, but it was a sure bet that one would come to visit if I had company in the house.

The experience of rebuilding changed my mind about some things. The words "quaint" and "rustic" were okay as long as they didn't mean crude and wasteful. Construction had to be elevated away from ground moisture and insects, and it had to be tight and efficient enough to conserve fuel and human energy. Those charming old multipane windows, for example, had to go. They looked pretty in the summer, but during a winter wind the drapes over those windows would actually flutter—there was little practical advantage in heating the outdoors.

By degrees, the cabin became a house. It lost some qualities and gained others. My plan changed as my experience grew, too. The screen porch I'd originally wanted became part of the house. I put the wood stove out there, because being in the same room with it would cook the life out of me. From there, it heats the entire house, and this winter the gas furnace hasn't been used at all. I gave up the screened porch and gained something more important.

When I was about halfway into the project, an old-timer in the area said, "You should have burned that place down and built from scratch." I knew what he meant. In the early days here, crude housing had been expendable, and locals would throw together a new place when the old one got run down. But when I'd started I was both too stubborn and too naive to have considered such a suggestion. Besides, I could not have afforded such a major expense, nor did I have the skills for such a big project. So, I learned as I went, and although it was inconvenient to live in a partially built house, at least I had a place to live.

I'm pleased with the result. The place grew with me, and it fits. It's suitable for my purposes, being neither too much, nor too little. And it reminds me of all the people who helped with the work and provided information and ideas. It is a human product. The skills of many individuals made it happen. Concepts from other buildings were adapted to this one, which represents my personal blend of rural and modern living.

As I look back, the part of the project that hurt the most was covering up the logs on the outside. Once the logs were covered, the place no longer had the charm of a cabin. But it had to be done to make the house livable and efficient. I can tell you what pleased me the most; too—getting in running water. It took eight years to acquire that convenience, and I spent a week or so afterward taking showers all day. That's an exaggeration, but it was sure nice to have plumbing. After having lived without it for so long, that little silver handle on the flush box was a marvel.

Each room has its own native wood. The main room is done in pine panelboards from trees cut north of Hovland when I was a boy. The boards had been stored in a shed all those years. Old Bill had cut the trees, and it was a lucky accident that I was able to purchase the boards from his estate. The cedar boards in the downstairs bedroom came from Hovland, too. They were prepared by Don, an excellent sawyer who specialized in cedar. The framing wood came from Otis. You could always count on him for good dimension lumber. It's covered up, but the house wouldn't hold together as well without that contribution.

Fancier types of panelling came from the Hedstrom mill in Grand Marais. I didn't use their good stuff when I was first learning, but now it has a place in my plan. The large upstairs bedroom is done in an interesting combination of matched cedar and pine panels from the mill.

Gust is the one who taught me to use stain and varnish. Without his guidance, I would not have dared to experiment with colors or tackle the more delicate finishing. It is slow, patient work, and it took a while before I was able to do it. At first I was in too much of a hurry.

Charlie helped with the wiring, and Cliff taught me framing, as did John and Gene. Pete showed me how to use glue, small nails, and plywood to beef up collar ties and make a tighter frame. The list of those who helped goes on and on.

The point I wish to make is that the house was not a solo effort. The effort came from many directions and many lives. I could claim self-reliance and independence, but I appreciate all the help that went into making this place.

The cabin, now a house, is where I live and work. I'm surrounded by the contributions that formed this structure, which is both a stimulus and a gift. Fixing up this place over the years, I've grown to see a side of people that is warm and familiar. Writing is somewhat lonely work, and for me in particular, it's good to remember the web of life and lives that adds meaning to my existence here. When I forget that, I'll end up writing for myself, alone.

I can show you a little of the meaning it has by telling you about a winter ritual of mine.

It's well after dark and the night is cold. I turn on the big hanging lamp in the main room, open the drapes, put on my coat, and go outside. I walk down to the lake. The cold is sharp, the snow creaks as I walk, the ice on Lake Superior groans and cracks as it freezes and expands. Overhead, the distant suns called stars flicker, giving no warmth. I take in the night scene until I feel cold, then I walk back toward the house. The main room, with the drapes open, is aglow. The mellow pine panelling gives the room a warm color and a warmer feeling. It looks inviting and comfortable against the snow drifted outside the windows. Standing in the cold, I look into the room and feel its warmth and peace. It's a reminder I need. When I go inside I'll be back home.

Afterword

Winter has many faces. It is dangerous and beautiful. It is blindingly obvious and profoundly mysterious. It is literary, historical, timeless, and temporal. The stillness of winter is the flow of life, which pauses as it gathers strength.

As a people, though, we tend to orient our lives toward spring and summer. We are attracted to youth, warmth, and color, often running from the face of winter, or seeking to blunt the ways it touches us. The fact that we run is human enough to understand, but it's a tragedy that we believe we lack the strength to face winter. We cling to summery times in our hearts, avoiding the chilly hint of unwanted change.

But I'm sure we do not really lack the strength to face change. The harshness of winter is not an end to life and loving. Indeed, the cold blast of winter may bring out the warmth in us, fostering enough real change to turn false spring into rebirth. It is ironic how we sometimes flee from that which might ultimately benefit us the most.

Doesn't winter offer us the most by demanding the most from us? Don't we come to value the warmth of cooperation, kindness, and the like by having experienced its absence? The external conditions of winter can be seen as mirrors to internal conditions of being human. Perhaps the worst form of winter is, indeed, a condition that resides within us. Call it a bitter winter wind which freezes fast on unpleasant memory. There it clings. Nothing will pass by that is not colored by chilling memory. No good news can be announced when energy goes into repeating the old, chill, bad news of the past.

Having written about winter camping and about winter, I've been aware, all along, that I've been writing about us. While most of my comments deal with the practical aspects of survival while tenting, I am as much concerned about the growth and survival of dynamic human spirits. I've no definition for human spirit and certainly no well-defined pathway for readers to follow. I have simply tried to suggest ways of forming a partnership with winter.

I've suggested, too, a view of life like that found in the Native American's Hoop. And I've suggested that much careful preparation can still have outcomes we've not anticipated. When taken by surprise, have we failed to be adequately prepared or are we being presented with new opportunity? I don't know. But I believe that the study of winter and its constraints adds perspective and potential to the process of filling out our lives. The constraints of winter are intellectual and emotional training grounds where we separate matters of survival from trivial concerns. The task (I think of it as a human adventure) goes best if one actually braves winter's environment, but you need never go camping to harvest winter's offerings.

Whichever your path, I wish you well. I hope you'll find, as I have, a winter reward where only a short while before you'd have never thought to look.

Notes

Notes

Notes

Notes

Checklist

ITEM	Checked	Rechecked
Clothing		
Long underwear & spares	_____	_____
Wool pants, suspenders, belt	_____	_____
Shirt	_____	_____
Handkerchief & spare	_____	_____
Snowmobile boots & spare liners	_____	_____
Ski boots, gaiters, overboots	_____	_____
Vest	_____	_____
Wool Jacket	_____	_____
Down Jacket & hood	_____	_____
Goggles or sunglasses	_____	_____
Chapstick	_____	_____
Wool socks & spares	_____	_____
Mitts, liners, & spares	_____	_____
Hat, wool cap, face mask	_____	_____
Quilted underwear set	_____	_____
Other_____	_____	_____
Other_____	_____	_____
Travel Equipment		
Skis & poles	_____	_____
Snowshoes	_____	_____
Wax kit, ski tip, etc.	_____	_____
Towing toboggan & poles	_____	_____
Push-bar	_____	_____
Foam blocks	_____	_____
Pack frame	_____	_____
Spare parts & tool bag	_____	_____
Other_____	_____	_____
Other_____	_____	_____
Camping Equipment		
4-person Eureka Timberlines	_____	_____
Timberline vestibules	_____	_____
Versa Tarp groundcloth	_____	_____
Steel spikes	_____	_____
Wind tarp or Versa Tarp	_____	_____

Tear out copy

ITEM	Checked	Rechecked
Cord	_____	_____
Candle lanterns & candles	_____	_____
Camp shovels	_____	_____
Axe & saw	_____	_____
Cooking grate	_____	_____
Fire Starter	_____	_____
Duluth No. 3 Cruiser packs	_____	_____
Coleman Peak stove, fuel, filter	_____	_____
Cook kit, silverware, etc.	_____	_____
Dishpan	_____	_____
Thermos & liner	_____	_____
Food pack *plus three days food*	_____	_____
Map, compass, etc.	_____	_____
Recreation (camera, fishing, etc.)	_____	_____
Liquid soap, matches, etc.	_____	_____
Other_____	_____	_____
Other_____	_____	_____

Sleeping Equipment

	Checked	Rechecked
Duluth No. 3 Cruiser packs (approx. 1 per person)	_____	_____
Sleeping bag/bags	_____	_____
Thermal liners	_____	_____
Foam pads (3 per 2 people)	_____	_____
Wool blanket or flannel cover	_____	_____
Other_____	_____	_____
Other_____	_____	_____

Automobile

	Checked	Rechecked
Jumper cables	_____	_____
Tire chains	_____	_____
Cold starting carb spray	_____	_____
Window scraper	_____	_____
Large shovel	_____	_____
Carriers	_____	_____
Other_____	_____	_____
Other_____	_____	_____

Tear out copy